Somewhere Out in the West
We'll Build a Sweet Little Nest

A NOVEL

by

Leota Korns

ISBN: 1-4033-3341-6 (e-book)
ISBN: 1-4033-3342-4 (Paperback)
ISBN: 1-4033-3343-2 (Dustjacket)

Library of Congress Control Number: 2002092115

This book is printed on acid free paper.

Printed in the United States of America
Bloomington, IN

1stBooks - rev. 09/26/02

CHAPTER 1

HANK BURBANK MEETS ARTHUR STAHLEK

The U.S.Home Secretary, Hank Burbank, made another Executive Order to do what he had not been able to get the States to do. He set up Regions. He and his staff worked the details out ahead of time. In the West the boundaries will fall more naturally along topographical or other natural indicators such as rivers, mountain ranges, basins, than State boundaries now do, which were set up in the East. And for this the inhabitants and voters were happy. But Burbank did not vacate the state governments. They were held accountable for carrying out his Executive Order No. 125.

At first the new changes addressed environmental concerns like questions of wildlife, endangered species, uses of national forests, land management, rivers, water storage and growth.

But the Order has left the citizen not knowing the geographical boundaries, that is which Region the citizen is occupying or to be more exact, who is making the laws or the regulations, that is, who is one's representative? Apparently the U.S. Home Office and now with the United States president's blessing, someone or ones have been appointed to make these regulations and laws by some unknown, to the citizen, layer of government. Not even the Federal Congress has a say. No state official has resigned. The State Legislature still meets but seems subject to the Region. And the Region is subject to _____?

The News Media is going along and so is the Education System. The News Media seems asleep whereas the Educational Complex seems to be alert and part of the change. The Education System will no longer be voted on locally. It is under the Region buried somewhere in government. The State Legislatures are at this time an unknown quantity. In the land management regulations there is rumor that in the near future only people owning land will have the right to vote and only if they allow their land to be managed by the Region and live according to this management. The economy had not been addressed in Executive Order No. 125.

The right to vote through land ownership managed by government is just a rumor and citizens cognizant with the rumor wonder just how Burbank and his party will try to pull it off. Burbank is making a trip out West and people like land owners, ranchers, developers are waiting. Of course, there's a large percentage of the citizens totally unaware and have been sensitized to saving the first promised changes in Executive Order 125 like wildlife, endangered species, rivers, national forests preserved for people on foot, and curtailing growth and development all over the West.

So it was with curious interest that Arthur Stahlek stood alone against the western sky, tall, intelligent, beautiful, a finely chiseled face, ears to the head, brunette yet. The Western hat framed his head like a monument. Broad shoulders, slim hips and body.

Arthur Stahlek took after his mother, Ida. He was not angular and thin as Matt, his father, when Matt was young. The nose is smooth and straight, not hump bridged as

Matt's whose complexion is also different—light and hair reddish blond.

Arthur's face was still smooth and the weight of years has not settled in his face and body. He stood alone on a rise on his grazing land, unirrigated, fragile with blades of vegetation spacing themselves. His black border collie, Bringum, stood by his master at ease, ready.

There were deep tire tracks made by circle turns in the dry powder soil. Art planned to bring these to the attention of the Home Secretary Burbank and inform him that it is his land but not his tire tracks.

The Home Secretary arrived with a cadre of Interior Home people. They disembarked and Burbank led. From the road he looked up at the man he will talk to about many things on the Western agenda. He viewed Arthur through three great strands of barbed wire measuring off the picture—one strand across Bringum, the second across Arthur's elbows and midriff, the third above the cowboy hat. A cumulus cloud floated across the sky. The hat brim shaded Arthur's eyes which were shielded by black horn rimmed glasses. Unlike Matt, Arthur's been educated with a degree in agriculture, soil and water conservation.

The long absence of rain, the dearth of vegetation, the powdered soil are clearly issues for both Arthur and Home Secretary, Hank Burbank.

The Home Secretary spoke first. "We could do with some rain!"

"Yes, Sir."

Art looked Burbank straight in the eye then scanned the cadre. Slowly he extended his

hand.   Burbank was ready.   A good firm shake
was made.

"We need the dam," Art said and his eye
contact was firm.

Burbank looked away.

Art moved his boot toe gently into the
powder earth.   Burbank's gaze followed Art's
toe.   "You can see how this soil was once
productive before our water rights were
legislated away.   The dam will settle many
claims for water.   The dry farmers here, the
New Mexico farmers who won't be asked to give
up what they took, the four Indian tribes'
treaties will be honored and fulfilled, the
area cities will not have to be abandoned.   It
makes sense."

Burbank made no response.

"The only thing we rent is the grass that
grows.   We furnish water, fences and

everything else. If anybody is going to take care of the land they need to have a feeling of being here."

Arthur's knowledge of the land was immediately evident as he pointed out western wheat grass, cheat grass, rabbit brush, greasewood, four-wing salt brush, and pack-rat nests. He knew every plant on the 13-square mile winter range that was a mixture of his private land, U.S. Interior Land, and acreage owned by the neighboring State of New Mexico.

"We have waited through the Viet Nam War, the Environmental Movement. The costs keep rising. It makes no sense to restore fish found elsewhere, which will conflict with the Fish and Game Department, and which were destroyed by the government previously. Our big problem is the Endangered Species Act. You owe it to all the citizens of this area, to all who come from all over the nation, the world, for vacationing and recreation to provide their needs of water. We expect you to fulfill building the dam passed and funded by Congress back in 1968."

Burbank did not answer.

Art's right arm moved in a circle up the rise following the tire tracks. "Some one with a Land Rover, perhaps, has been up here. If I'd done this, I'd lose my lease. We have to be careful. We have to take care of the land. It's becoming a situation where we have no control, no rights over our land. Taxes but no rights. We might as well be in Russia."

"I don't perceive it as that bad," Burbank said, looking on up the rise. In the distance there was sage and further up small juniper and pinon. "We have to be responsible for all

9

people, not just a few ranchers," Burbank said and brought his gaze back straight into Art's for a brief moment. Then he looked away again and said, "The Federal lands belong to all citizens and the lands' water must be protected."

"How?" Art queried.

"By keeping it on Federal lands!" Burbank answered defiantly and impatiently.

"But if the water runs off, how you going to keep it? If it's down below then what use is your Federal water rights! I can't see what you're trying to do."

Burbank looked at Art again and it was clear he did not want to pursue the subject. "We have other people to call on. Will you be at the meeting tonight?"

"I certainly intend to. We built this ranch one cow at a time. I move cattle off the New

Mexico range for the entire growing season to let it rest. You can't force the land."

As they left, one of the cadre looked back over his shoulder and quipped, "Maybe you should just quit then."

CHAPTER 2
BURBANK'S SPEECH

On the speaker's platform were the four attendants of Burbank—news, office, speech writer and public relations along with the regional water board president, the Luna County Electric Company chairman, three Indian Tribal leaders, the president of the Colorado Anglo-Indian State College, the president of the University Professors' Association of the College, the Luna City mayor, the governor.

On the front row were some eighteen media people—radio, T.V., newspaper—from six surrounding towns, all having an interest and neighboring Federal lands, and all there to hear for themselves progress on the dam affecting the entire area, plus the large Colorado state and capitol media.

Down front early come, early seated, were all the interests—the several bank presidents, one current large developer, many well known ranchers, attorneys working in development, real estate and water, surveyors, engineers, architects, planners, town and country people.

People carrying placards were all around the edges of the auditorium, walking up and down the aisles, turning their signs frontward and rearward for all to see. There seemed to be no restrictions on the free speech exhibited on the college campus.

All necessary introductions were made. The college president, introduced Burbank who jumped up to the microphone and told the audience that he'd been in the area visiting with people and talking to as many folks as possible since early morning and was now crowded for time to catch his plane and continue his western trip.

Getting serious, he began. "We must protect our Ancient Forests. Ancient Forests are home to many of our endangered species. When they're gone there will be no more and our lives will be diminished. Therefore, my order of a severe cutback in logging will not be rescinded. And no more controlled burns! We're going to protect what God gave to us—our Ancient Forests."

"Whoopie! Hooray!" the placard bobbed as James Murray danced with it.

"The same goes for sheep and cattle in our forests. Our forests will be returned to the people and not the privilege of the few."

"COWS POINT OF DISCHARGE IS OUR STREAMS!" Egbert Easterly with a small group of friends cheered and waived a placard.

"Federal water on our National Forests will also be protected.

"We will be building more trails. There is a need for trails through private lands to furnish connection to the trails which are scheduled to be built. We will need deeded private lands for connecting the trails in our lands so that more people can use our forests."

"Make them deed their land!" Tom Walker waved his placard to and fro: WALK! DON'T POLLUTE!

"How can we put that into law? That private land can be forced to deed property for our trails?" Matt Stahlek asked.

"I will have to get back with you on that!" Burbank said and continued. "In order to accomplish all of this we must cut back on development and it's call for water and the loss of our open spaces."

DEVELOPERS RAPE! "I tell you I'm an environmentalist!" Darth Damuel called out. He had bought a choice lot in Quiet Mountain and built a large home.

"The same with mining. Old claims must be surrendered."

Burbank concluded, reaffirming he was happy to have had this day with people of this region. He was sure there were questions and he would stay longer and answer all he could.

Arthur Stahlek was the first. "But the forests are managed now for multiple use. How's that different from what you're going to do?"

"The cattle are ruining the riparian areas. They're polluting our rivers and streams. We're set to reclaim these areas."

Matt Stahlek said, "There's been more than a century of cattle in the high country and mountain water was clean. Now that we have thousands of backpackers our water is becoming polluted and you want to add more!"

"I have not been notified that backpackers pollute."

"Our local foresters say that covering their pollution with a spadeful of dirt washes away with the first rain into the stream. You get giardia and now the wildlife have it too."

"It has not been called to my attention," and Burbank turned away from Matt to another part of the audience and recognized the next speaker.

The next speaker was Elmer Jarvis, the logger and heavy equipment construction operator. "The forests are becoming tinder boxes, ready to explode with old and rotting timber on the floor. Why don't you want good fire protection?"

TREE MURDERERS! James Murray held his placard way up high.

"Fires are nature's way of cleansing the forest."

"But who benefits?"

"New plant life."

There was an old miner down on the front row. Judith Sandstrom, getting there late from Quiet Mountain, the development she and her husband, John, were doing, had to stand in the rear of the hall. She could barely see the head of the old miner. There seemed to be friends on either side of him to support him in his defense against Burbank's order on stoppage of mining in the mountains. To Judith there seemed to be a history here that she was not familiar with.

The old miner was shaken by Burbank's words.
He lashed out, "You won't take that claim away
from me! I have put my life in it! You'll
have to take it over my dead body!"

It caused a stir and Burbank was not so
ready with his axe words. The friends around
the old miner, from what Judith could see
seemed to be trying to quiet him. Their arms
seemed to be around him in a mixture of
comfort and support for his claim, a mixture
of patience as if there was a better, more
efficient way to stand up to the Federal
government than individual lashing. The old
miner was not easily quelled. He kept trying
to get on his feet and to threaten and Judith
could hear the shock and dismay in his voice.
Her heart went out to him. She and John had
taken the same beatings over developing Quiet
Mountain. She would like to unite with the

miner, comfort him but she was too far away. She looked around in search of someone to express her dismay, shock and outrage. Albert Brown, a science prof at the college, round and solid, giving off an air of complete self-satisfaction, was nearby but before she could voice her feelings to him, he was saying, not unhappily to her and to those around him, concerning the miner, "He will just have to give up and go with the greater good!" He then smiled excessively and benevolently. It struck Judith that the science professor had a history too in the content of Burbank's speech. She closed her mouth and knew the new environmental movement, with all its attending science, education and media coverage, was frightening and greater than she ever thought it could be. She knew that for most of the professors it was a total switch from what

John prized—nature. She knew their favorite pastime was putting on their shorts and with an iced cocktail, mow their beautiful lawns. She knew that only a very few of them could appreciate John and her desire to live in the midst of nature on a mountain. She had been told, "Quit it! Come into town and live like us!" It would have been the death of her and John to give up Quiet Mountain.

She looked back at the old miner down front and to her surprise someone she didn't know was squatting in front of him and writing information on a notepad and then the stranger snapped a couple of pictures with the camera he had around his neck. She would certainly try to get acquainted with this photographer to find out where he stood and came from.

The crowd had now thinned and a collection of ranchers lingered and began to talk to each

21

other. Arthur Stahlek said to Elmer Jarvis and his top foreman, Dennis Cameron, "Well he said nothing about the dam but he knows how I feel because I told him today. He visited me on the ranch. He's trying to take all the water for the Feds. I don't see how he's going to do that and not build storage. I think he's got one hellavan appetite."

Elmer Jarvis answered, "Without a doubt! But did you hear on the news this evening that the courts have overturned his logging constraints on cleaning up the forest floors?"

"No, I was in the field until sunset."

"It looks like we'll have another two years' work before doomsday!" Dennis added. "Maybe we need one more organization to fight the Feds."

"Yeah! Maybe we'll have to," Matt added and there was reluctance in his voice.

"Let's talk about this again at the next Farm Bureau meeting. Why don't you two fellows come? Be my guests!"

Jarvis nodded his head thoughtfully.

"I'll keep you informed. I'll call you," Art said.

CHAPTER 3
QUIET MOUNTAIN

It was the quiet of fall in the Rockies. The heat of summer and the deerflies were gone. The atmosphere stilled. The bright sun glinted off the metallic waters of the Luna River.

The water tank perched high up on the mountain but there was much more of Selene Mountain above the tank. From the height of the tank you looked in the distance toward the Moctezuma Range. The sun hung low in the Southern Sky like a solitary jewel. With the sun back of you, you could discern the road cut horizontally across the face of Bertha Peak, leading to the Alma J silver mine, 13,000 plus feet elevation.

On up higher the Ponderosa were bull size, and older than the arrival of the English in

North America. Their needles shimmered in the sunlight and moved gently, giving off more shimmering. If one studied the trees well, you could discover a blue spruce or Norway spruce at your elbow, stretching skyward from a field of gambel oak. If room enough, the juniper grows large and round as a balloon. The trail upward was put there at the turn of the century, by timber harvesters and mining prospectors. It wound in and around Quiet Mountain, the mountain homesites John and Judith Sandstrom were developing on Selene Mountain. If kept clean of oak, and groves of Ponderosa swaying in the wind, striking one another and falling across the trail like barricades, one could drive their four-wheel many places on Selene Mountain.

By late October an early snow burned off the peaks of the Moctezumas and the oak was turning yellow-orange. The deciduous trees in the green, watersmooth floor of the valley will turn yellow in a week. The high, thin air exhilarates. Hubris was strong in the fall of the year.

The green water tank sat in place. The backhoe worked on the five foot deep trench in which to lay the water line to connect the water main and tank below. From the green tank the backhoe worked straight down the mountain, over a ledge, turning up boulders repeatedly. The shovel slid off one boulder, lifted, backed down, dug in and uncovered the next. The backhoe now tilt to its side, fixed between a pine and a boulder. It made several tries to get at the large rock. It tilt more. Elmer Jarvis, the construction owner, watched the efforts of the young operator try to save the pine and get the boulder loose.

Judith Sandstrom watched with Jarvis. It will be either the boulder or the pine. The backhoe leaned precariously, held up by the root system of the pine.

The backhoe stopped its efforts. Jarvis addressed Judith.

"Is that pine important to you?"

Judith looked at the forest. She knew the approximate age of the pine from Steinhoff, the Colorado Forester, coring a similar size pine. She looked past one dying from beetles to one with mistletoe, all of similar size, and to all the many others.

She thought of the added time.

Jarvis said, "We can maybe save the tree but it will take some time and doing."

Judith wonderd if that can be so. Really? Would the backhoe overturn?

"Take the tree out," she said.

The backhoe pushed the tree aside. It fell to the ground. It did not now look imposing nor threatening. It was not big enough for lumber. It would make firewood but with Darth Damuel pulling up monuments, markers and stakes, and exciting the other lot owners, it would be better to not give the tree away and beg attention. Let it return to the soil, she thought, and wondered if this was waste or returning nutrients.

Judith walked down the mountain, picking her way around the heaped up soil and boulders of the open trench to where the trail down remained untouched by the backhoe, and lay lovely in the shade of the pines. The trench was steep and bouldered, but when covered back will be used by hikers and horses. She loved it now and will love it when water runs beneath it. She envisioned a dream. A dream cf sharing. A dream of what she's felt with John as they rested on boulders on the mountain, planning their future with the mountain. A dream of solitude. A dream of supreme quiet. Of a southwest breeze through pine needles and branches. Of a hawk and then another circling overhead searching for their evening meal. A true yearning for an uncertain ideal of peaceful nature, a graciousness founded upon wisdom, tolerance, reason and principle. A false and tricky dream.

The trail turned into an old worn two-wheel, rutted logging road running along the mountain's side. It will be given a Quiet Mountain name. Her jeep was parked along this old lumber road. She drove the jeep down hill, around the bend, while gazing straight ahead at the mountains across the valley floor and far beyond and felt again her breath taken by their beauty. As she descended into the platted land she notices more stakes and monuments missing. She drove on around the bend where the pump house and lower tank were situated. Something flashing red protruded from behind the wellhouse. As she drove nearer she could discern the lettering of her realtor.

She questioned how his sign got behind the wellhouse.

A county sheriff's patrol car surfaced from the bend below. It pulled to a stop alongside Judith's jeep. Beside the deputy sat Jim Hurst, Judith and John's realtor.

"I'm looking for my sign!" Hurst called out.

"What's that behind the wellhouse!" Judith answered.

The undersheriff and Jim got out and examined the sign. It was Hurst's and was fractured with a beer can stuck in the break. The frame was twisted, torn loose from the sign and looked to have been thrown behind the wellhouse.

Hurst shook his head. He looked angry, shocked, and hurt.

"That fellow, Damuel, phoned my office. I brought the undersheriff with me. I was afraid of trouble."

Judith was also troubled and hurt. "You can't sell your property. Yet they demand you improve it."

"They want a damned city up here!"

"I know it," she said. Yet she didn't know it. She couldn't understand it. She couldn't voice her confusion.

"I'm going back to my office and see what's there. Then I'll go to my attorney, Francine. Damuel is pulling up survey markers. We'll have to get a restraining order." She felt the dread in her bones.

"Something's gotta be done!" Hurst said.

Judith followed Hurst down past Damuel's house, three stories, wrapped with decks and balconies on the upper levels.

Quiet Mountain had come a long way since John and Judith first purchased the land and friends picnicked with them higher up beyond the upper tank and suggested they build summer cabins.

`"But move down every winter a mile or so into town?" That seems like a lot of trouble, Judith thought. And one by one permanent homes were built and John and Judith had formed a strong governing body to guide Quiet Mountain.

Judith stopped at the post office and picked up her mail.

There was a letter from Damuel. She twisted and tore the end of the envelope, peeling it open, and pulled out his letter. It was a copy of a letter he'd written to Francine.

"Rest assured all signs over 1 x 2 feet will come down," the letter read in answer to Francine's request. "The Quiet Mountain sign will be removed by the 10th of the month."

That means the identification sign. The sign that tells where Quiet Mountain is. Vulnerable! No identification sign on a secluded county road! How would she ever advertise where Quiet Mountain is? How would she direct people? She knew Damuel's plan.

She still had trouble coming to terms with the evil in others.

She took the letter to Francine's office. He had already read it. He seemed unmoved by the letter. Judith was alarmed. Taking down the identification sign could not be tolerated. It was like closing Quiet Mountain down. Hiding it in a closet.

"I can't live with the sign gone!" she said.

Francine studied her.

"It won't be that bad," he commented.

"Enough harm's been done to the reputation of Quiet Mountain! I'm advertising it. Prospects must be able to find it! The tenth is the second day from today! I can't afford a new sign every week for Damuel to take down!"

"We can get a temporary restraining order."

"Get a permanent one!"

34

Francine studied her more. He was a good attorney. He knew she's dependent upon him for know-how with the law. And she knows he gauges his client's emotion with the facts.

"How soon can we get it?" she asked, hating the whole mess.

"I can't get it done today. The courthouse closes in a little. I'll do it first thing in the morning."

"Then what is the next step?"

"You'll have to serve it on him. Either by mail or in person."

"Mail is too slow. I'll take it to him."

"I'll call your office as soon as I have the order. If you go in person you need someone with you to witness delivery."

"I don't think we should convey the water system, regardless of what the Veteran's Administration asks!"

Francine spoke with resolve which surprised her. "I guess you won't!"

"We don't need the VA," she said.

"I'll write another letter to Damuel."

CHAPTER 4

THE BLUE SPRUCE TREE

Six volunteers equipped with long handled shovels, axes, cutter and pick mattocks, and spades approached their three mile assignment in the building of the Inter-Mountain Trail. It was very early at break of dawn. They scouted the area again, having seen the extent of it, where their three mile ends yesterday. To take the trail upward they now realized a tall beautiful, stately blue spruce was directly in the path.

"Let's scout this out," Egbert said.

Egbert walked up from the spruce but a boulder 40 ft. high was in the way. Stan scouted below the spruce.

"We lose altitude this way. It will take a lot of cutting and lengthen our section," Stan said.

"Hey! If we were sawyers!" Roland called.

"Or loggers," Connie answered.

"Or lumber jacks," Hubert threw in.

Egbert laughed. "May I finish? If we were sawyers we could cut the spruce down."

"But none of us has ever cut a tree," Roland said.

"Yeah but none of us has ever cut a trail in the Colorado Rockies either!" Stan said.

"Yeah!" Hubert echoed.

"Besides it would leave a stump and be disturbing for hikers wanting a wilderness experience. At least it would be for me," Connie added.

"Let's dig it out!" Stan readied his mattock.

"Yeah. Then fill in, cover the spot, and give the effect of original nature undisturbed except for walking feet," Egbert embellished.

"Besides I don't like chain saws," Stan exclaimed.

"And the damned noise they make," Connie reinforced him.

By noon the down slope side of the tree was dug out and much of the tree's exposed roots had been severed. They worked on the uphill side, saving earth for refill. Stones nestled tightly and were encompassed in the root system. In spite of the best of care, sparks flew from the stones as the axes struck the spruce roots. Much of the root system was severed but the spruce stood tall and skyward. The cutters went deeper and cut underneath the tree, the tap root.

Stan had brought a rope. He threw the rope to a lower pine, leaving an end free to pull. Egbert took the other end and went to the uphill side of the Blue Spruce, stood in the fresh dug earth, and felt in the thick abundant spruce needles for the trunk, maneuvered the rope around the trunk and climbed back out of the freshly dug earth.

"Ready!" he called.

Four started pulling the rope They did not affect the spruce. It was a beauty. Well formed. Rising to a point 60 feet above them. It was decided to pull in strokes. They appointed a caller and now pulled in strokes. Their pulls did not matter to the spruce. Then six more arrived assigned to the three mile beyond.

"What gives?" they called.

"We've got to get this spruce out of the way of the trail."

"That's a beauty!" They jumped out of the jeep and looked up in the blue sky to the top of the spruce.

"Let's help."

"Yeah, this should be interesting!"

They fanned out to each end of rope. It made a big difference. Little by little they saw a slight movement in the spruce. The mighty spruce gave the volunteers confidence. They gave the spruce tree more concerted effort.

"It's beginning!" Egbert called out.

There was the snap of a root breaking.

The spruce responded to the pulling strokes. The top began to quiver. Another root heaved up but was still grounded.

"Keep it up!" called Stan.

The pullers exerted more energy.

"Where will it fall?" shouted Connie.

"I don't know!" Egbert said.

"Stop!" Jenny, one of the three females, shouted.

41

"It could fall on us! We want it to fall in that open space. If it falls towards us it will take this pine and leave another stump," Connie said.

They studied the situation. More rope was tied to the spruce and then pulled through another pine over to the left of the blue spruce, making a triangle of the two pines and the spruce. Half of the pullers moved over to the left pine and the caller called out the strokes, shouting "more to the left!" "to the right!" The spruce jolted both ways.

"It's coming!" called Egbert. "Pull together now! Together! Left! Right!" More snapping and upheaval of roots and the tree begins to tilt irreversibly downward. The stroking mounted, the tree snaps more.

"It's falling! Left pull hard! Get loose!"

The spruce crashed to the earth just missing the right pine and the right pullers. It was loaded like a christmas tree with small soft spruce cones and they laid in a bundle on the ground—branches, needles, and cones. Beautiful even in death.

"That was exciting!" Jenny exclaimed.

"I never dreamed I'd come to Colorado and pull down a giant blue spruce!" Laurie answered.

"Me neither," Connie said.

"Cutting the roots of Democracy!" Stan philosophized.

"Yeah! It's through competing!" Egbert gave the epitaph.

"Maybe others will now have a chance!" Hubert declared righteously.

"Good job!"

The second group got into their jeep and went on to the next three miles of trail assigned to them.

The first of the hawks started circling, looking for their evening meal, oblivious to the fate of the Blue Spruce.

"What are we going to do with it?"

"Wonder if you could get a house out of it?"

"Did anyone bring a saw?"

"Loggers would be jealous. Angry as hell!"

"Mad as hell, I'd say."

"We need hand saws. Cross cuts."

"We need to limb it fast. Get the slash down where the snows will bury it."

"Let's saw it into firewood and skid it back along the trail. Get a tarp to skid it."

They left for their three cars parked down by the creek, returning with at least a half dozen cross cut caws and a portable steno, tapes and a tarp. They worked like busy beavers limbing the spruce until only the huge log was left. Now they cut every available piece of wood for their earth stoves. At last they cut the small limbs into short lengths for the snows to press down into the earth.

They scouted the road and surround for other users of the National Forest. They were alone enough to enjoy some good rock and roll. The music thumped/drummed/beat loud on the nervewracking off beat. There was beer and joy. They had cut a giant spruce. It will be a treasured memory. It will be a special secret. One they can relate on rare occasions to comrades of similar experiences and nerve.

Two tarps were mustered. The woods people needed a lot of beer and muscle and many trips to get the firewood down to the trucks. They posted a lookout as they had no permit for firewood cutting either.

In the evening they smoked marijuana and let their memories weave into the haze. Weary and satisfied. Nothing in their lives would ever match digging out the giant spruce with shovels and pick axes. They had come form New York, New Jersey, Florida, California, the Front Range and locally.

"We've got a secret."

"Yeah. Let's not lose it nor each other."

"Each year we should come back and renew our acquaintance and walk the Inter-Mountain Trail."

"If it weren't for the boulder, I don't think in the future we could ever find the spot where the spruce grew."

When Egbert was three or four he was in the Super Mart with his mother, Mrs. Easterly. Judith and Johnny were still rubbing noses. Johnny was about six. They were in the Super Mart approaching the meat department in the rear of the store and Egbert and his mother approached it too.

Egbert's family were newcomers to Luna City and were living in one of the newly designed homes of the Fifties which were all on one level, built so the mother, without help, could birth and raise four to six children. In this regard the kitchen was the central place where the mother could care, nurture, and organize all activities and keep an eye on them. These were the baby boom years. Egbert's family had by this time four children all under the age of nine.

Egbert's father had a good job. There was money enough for the latest and especially so in the new psychology of raising children. More modern really than Dr. Spock. There were a number of families in this social group. Most of these types of parents had no control over their children, felt inadequate for the new parenting role, and weekly sought psychological guidance. Their homes were very often without order nor anyone having selfworth. It was a period of wiping the slate clean in the formations of their children's childhood so that their children entered adulthood without the emotional scars that were known in all the older generations.

Judith and Johnny advanced to the meat counter when Egbert's mother let go of her grocery cart, nearly full of groceries, to select some cuts of meat. Little Egbert saw his chance. He reached for the carton of a dozen eggs on the top of the pile in his mother's cart and sailed it to the floor. In his haste to complete the act he scratched a finger on the metal of the grocery cart enough to draw blood.

The Super Mart dispatched help to clean up the eggs and to keep traffic flowing. Egbert's mother grabbed hold of Egbert's finger and began pressing and squeezing the blood out while Egbert threw a good fit of kicking, squalling and twisting away. Mrs. Easterly dragged the battler to a sink in the far rear behind the meat counter where she could run water on the cut which was the most important thing of the whole event-protecting the child at any cost.

Johnny looked at Judith and shook his head. Judith smiled and agreed with him.

Egbert did not receive punishment nor discipline even though it was evident he had done something to be punished for. He only received the same dose of protection and throughout his life Egbert thirsted for a taste of punishment or discipline. Once when he was seven he brought a belt to his mother and asked her to whip him. He had heard other children bragging about their old-fashioned whippings and he wanted to know how it felt. But he was disappointed. His mother replied, "I'm not allowed to hit you." So the thirst remained with him and also the feeling of being set aside—special.

Later in the night the cutters drove back to the scene of their crime to the spot where the spruce tree stood tall and proud. A moonless night with billions of stars in the firmament. An awesome sight. They retraced their day, walking down the slope where the giant fell, sitting on the boulder, trying to comprehend their immense accomplishment too awesome for words except they wondered if they'd done their part to help Burbank make the changes he wanted.

CHAPTER 5
NIGHT IN THE HOT SPRINGS

Judith picked up the permanent restraining order from Francine and took an eye witness companion to deliver it to Darth Damuel who wasn't home. They hurried to the post office before closing and mailed it, certified, special, restricted delivery with return receipt showing to whom, date and addressee's address.

Then on the weekend John suggested they needed a change and they went up into the Moctezuma's to the Swiss Village, Weisbaden, to take the natural steam baths and get away from Quiet Mountain.

The hot springs were in a cave back into the mountain, a steam bath created by a spring of hot water coming up from the earth's interior and the cold snow water trickling down from the ceiling of the cave. They sat in large cement pools and let the steam work on them, getting out often as the pool's rules dictated to cool off, dry off, and get a massage if desired or go outside to the hot pool.

Judith and John had done it all and moved into the hot pool built at the end of the deck. There were a number of people in the pool. Elmer Jarvis noticed Judith and introduced his wife, Joyce, and Dennis and Alma Cameron.

The pool was very comfortable with hot springs water of 86 degrees under a full October moon, peaking its face above the 14,000 feet peaks, that surround Weisbaden Village high in the Rockies.

Judith soon became mesmerized watching Alma Cameron in the hot springs water. Alma had a perfect heart-shaped face and smoothly contoured body. It soon became evident that Alma was the glue that binds. Binds her, her husband, Dennis, and their children, a family of ten. Judith watched and listened to Alma's heroic story as Alma, her hair precisely done up on top of her head, her hands paddlling and fluttering gently as she moved about in the water. In a month will be Thanksgiving by the calendar, but it was Thanksgiving tonight for the Camerons in the hot mineral springs pool, out under millions of stars in the Rockies. There they visited in the pool, Alma and Dennis Cameron, and Dennis' boss, Elmer Jarvis and wife Joyce, and Judith and John Sandstrom.

The Camerons had left Chicago to look for work. They had been in Colorado only three months. Alma was enthused and certain of the good fortune, and good fortunes to come, in their move to Colorado. "Dennis had been out of work for a long, long time. In the plumbing and heating business. There were ten cf us living off $1,000 a year in odd jobs and food stamps. That's $1,000 a year per person," Alma said as she kept moving slowly in the placid warm mineral water.

"We were in the bread and soup lines and they handed out two thousand, five hundred packages but there were four thousand five hundred people. They said they'd go get more."

Judith could see the whole experience was still a shock to Alma who kept moving and paddling her hands slowly and lovingly in the warm water as she talked. It crossed Judith's mind that we are over-produced in farm products. She thought of the distribution but found no answer.

Dennis spoke. "All automobile related industries were shutting down. A transmission plant with a half million square feet of space was closed." He named many others. "The industries are in a squeeze between the clean-up demands of environmentalists, high union labor and high utility rates. They can't make it."

"Industry is moving south," Alma said. "The South is giving them incentives. No taxes and free land. And the labor is cheaper. That way they can do their environmental clean-up and still make a profit."

"The employment in Cleveland, Toledo, Detroit, Pittsburgh, and now the Iron Range in Minnesota is horrible!" Dennis exclaimed.

"One day we were crying. It had come to that. The next day Dennis said, 'I think I'll drive to town and buy a Denver newspaper. I believe there's an ad for a job for me in that paper.'"

Alma with her hair still intact on top of her head, wading and dipping her smoothly contoured body into the soothing water, said, "I thought, Good night! two miles to town to buy a newspaper. I thought of the 50 cents or so and the gasoline. We were counting every penny."

Judith visualized the scene and listened.

"I said, 'Well if you feel that strongly go, and do it.' We are born again Christians. We talk over everything."

Dennis broke in, "She means we keep in touch with the Lord."

John recapitulated. "You talk things over with God."

Alma answered. "Yes, I used to pray and feel nothing. Now I pray and feel something and I let God guide me. It is a spirit-filled experience."

Alma swished the warm water with her extended hands and arms. Elmer and Dennis were big, tall, strong men, open and sometimes chiding Alma. Once they teased her of her naivete about John Denver. They were both willing to share their spirituality with John and Judith.

"Anyway, Dennis drove to town and got the paper. The first ad didn't answer. He called another that sounded right for us and that's how we met Joyce and Elmer. It was the greatest thing that ever happened to us. They are spirit-filled Christians too." Elmer, who had been listening to the Camerons tell their story anew to Judith and John, broke in, "Yes, everything in my business sense and experience told me not to hire a man who'd been out of work for months and on food stamps, but I did it anyway."

Alma said, "We left everything and came out. All appliances, furniture, the house. I don't know when we'll ever sell that house."

Elmer reassured, "They'll find something to do to take the place of heavy industry."

Judith said, "Maybe high technology."

The Camerons and Jarvises acceded uncertainly.

John said, "Last night I read in Business News hi tech jobs will never pay what the union labor of heavy industry paid. And the Business News article said hi tech jobs could be just as dull and boring."

Elmer and Dennis looked quickly at John and then said quietly, "Maybe more so."

Returning to moving out to Colorado, Dennis said, "Then the problem was to find a house which would house ten people." "And again against my better judgement," Elmer confessed, "I rented them a house for ten people and now I'm on my second trip with them showing them Colorado."

"All of our children came with us," Alma said, "and all have found jobs. My oldest is taking care of wealthy people and they just love her. My son-in-law has found good work. My next, age nineteen, is working but she intends to go back and get her R.N. Then I have a sixteen year old and she's finishing high school next year. My youngest is nine. He's in Ms. Carver's class."

"What about you, Elmer and Joyce, how many children do you have?" John asked.

"Only two. One son and one daughter. Our son is in school in the East."

"We have only one son," John said.

"It's wonderful to know a large family with children of good quality," Joyce said.

The Cameron's happiness and utter wonder spred out over the pool and the starlight and moonlight added a magic. The moon had almost achieved it's zenith.

"What a wonderful evening," Judith exclaimed, surmounting her own worries. "Your message from," and she paused, then said, "the universe that there was an ad for you in the Denver Post reminds me of a dream I had the night before we got Quiet Mountain approved by the County Commissioners."

"Tell us your dream," Alma pled.

"Go ahead," John urged.

Judith waited, weighing values in her head related to how much should others know about her, how much vulnerability could she live with and survive, and Quiet Mountain too. But the joy here in the moonlight at 9,500 feet in the Rockies with the higher peaks rimming the setting, the heat of the mineral water from deep inside the earth, the Hand of God showing in these people's lives, all these things overcame her fears on this particular night.

"It was the night before Quiet Mountain was approved by the county commissioners," she repeated. "The hot breath of the no-growthers could be felt upon our necks. It should have been a worrisome dream," she remembered, "but instead I dreamed John and I were on a vacation, camping out in a broad canyon where there were Indian ruins in the cliffs, a small stream, horseback trails and riding, and walking also.

"On the other side of the cliffs was a large dome of a mountain. The dome was smooth granite with no trees. The dome formed and rounded upward tree high but higher up cleared itself of trees which commenced again to the left of the dome at the top.

"We, John and I, were to go up this dome. A line of people were lined up to go up the dome. I wondered how on earth we were going to accomplish it. As I perplexed this problem I saw a bunch of horses to the right at the stream side, drinking water, their long necks stretched from shoulder high right down to the water. They were all taking very long drinks, once every now and then flicking off a fly with their tails.

"When the horses finished drinking, they formed themselves into a single file and walked along the stream towards us and the others waiting to go up the granite dome. There was no apparent leader in the horses and no one supervising them. They came to where the people were lined up and walked into the worn path in front of the people. It was a single path a foot to eighteen inches deep from wear. And when each horse stopped, the scarp above the worn path made it easy to cet atop the horse, and one by one we got on the horses' backs. The horses went directly to the dome and when the dome steepened the horses began to lay against it and we instinctively lay against the horse, leaving nothing up from the horse as to hinder its crawl. We laid against the horse so as to become one with the horse. A part of their legs, their hind quarters, their long necks up against the dome. Their skins became shiny and damp with sweat. I could see my sorrel horse's muscles crawl like snake skin.

"We came to a small indentation in the dome and there was a deformed sprig of a tree, old, but still trying to establish itself. The tree gave me comfort to be there and last so long. I felt I could hang onto it if no help came. I felt I could not go either up or down the dome without the help of the horses. The sorrel horse I was riding made movements to indicate he wanted me to get off which I did. And I reached for the deformed sprig. About that time a small gray mare approached and took the sorrel's place and I crawled upon the back of the small gray mare and we continued up the dome united in horse skin.

"When we got to the top of the dome there was a barbed wire fence and it was built close to the ground. There seemed to be no present reason, nor no use for the fence as you could walk around either end of it. But it was unquestionably there. Further, I was the only one who had to get under the fence. There seemed to be no reason yet unquestionably this was required of me. The gray mare stretched out on the ground and showed me how to make myself small enough to snake under intact a six inch clearing of the fence. I got down to commence the feat and the other climbers were also coaching me, and encouraging me. I finally made it, carefully pulling my legs out last and careful of my skin. As I was gathering myself to stand up I saw John walking away from me to my left toward the forest of trees. I tried to call him back. I couldn't get a sound to come. I was shocked and I was reaching toward him, my face contorted in a cry that couldn't come out. As I was watching John disappear into the trees I became aware that my little gray mare was also leaving, following the other horses to the right to a path down the mountain beyond the granite dome. I knew the horses were going down to bring up another group of people. I wanted to tell the horse we could stay and explore the ridge but it was useless to talk to the predestined horse. And the people were leaving, following their own destinies.

"I knew I would soon be alone. But as I fully stood up, a shaggy haired hippy, neither too old nor too young, was walking up from the other side of the mountain. As he approached he held out his hand to me. I took it and we began walking to the right on the ridge of the mountain. We could see far into the distances and see ridge after ridge. I did not need to tell him how hard the climb was for I knew he also had climbed. We walked on exploring and there was no fear."

They had listened intently to Judith's dream. She wished someone would tell her what it meant.

"The feeling I had from the dream was complete and total calm" she said. "And then we went before the county commissioners the next day to present Quiet Mountain."

John said, "I feel awe when I hear her dream."

Alma shook her lowered head. "It is a powerful dream," she said.

And for a while the dream carried a spell over the group and they were silent. Judith wandered what the dream truly meant. She went over many aspects of her life lining them up to see if they might fit the dream. She remembered when she stood on the edge of the bench at Quiet Mountain and surveyed the whole—the watersmooth valley, the early snow on the Moctezumas, the straight rising sandstone to the right, and the anxious turmoil of mountains to the left. It was a dizzying sensation. John was off with the realtor finding a boundary. She wondered if he had time to pause here and see this scene.

She could not believe she might possibly become connected to it. She had come unwillingly to this country, believing that she would be coming to a flat desert-like terrain as in Eastern Colorado. She realized now that God had led her to the most beautiful area of the Rockies. She stood there on the ledge with the bench area behind her and tried to get her breath, tried to envision the strange possibility of owning this spot. It was too much to accommodate at one time. Let it materialize less it carry a hidden disappointment.

Leota Korns

She knew it was true that they could possibly buy it. Within a month they put money down and began exploring their mountain while waiting six more months for the survey of the property to be finished. Daily at the close of college they rushed to the mountain to begin walking and recording each day's new discoveries. Sometimes they walked through narrow crevices, their shoes barely managing between upthrusted boulders, sometimes the discovery of a beautiful tall balsam, sometimes a grove of giant pines too close together to survive next spring's wind, sometimes a large rounded indentation from a meteorite, sometimes an average boulder up higher in the property with somewhat settled landscape around it, sometimes close to the top ridge of sandstone and the broken upheaval left from its uplift, a boulder as large as a house and flat on top for sunbathing. One day they scaled the wall of the top sandstone facing. Judith's nephew, Earl, home from Viet Nam scaled the wall and called down to them that he had spotted the corner marker and coming down the wall Judith watched his feet handling the rock slide, hopping upwards from one rock to the next as they rolled down under his feet. And all three of them exploring until after dark, separated, and Judith taking off running down the mountain to where she thought the car was parked without the slightest knowledge of the terrain she was running, the excitement putting wings on her feet.

Then the seriousness of developing. Filling the bathtub with gallon upon gallon of water to see how many gallons a bath tub took, trying to estimate how many baths could be obtained from one and a half gallons per minute yield when the klutzie well driller ran out of cable. And going down to Beaver Creek and hauling water up the mountain to water some plantings and settling for just dreaming of water on the mountain.

The disbelief when John finally obtained a reliable well driller who would chance a well on Selene Mountain, a mountain without a huge snow pack. With the help of a geologist to tell them in what formation they'd find water, they drilled and got a supply in one well enough for the whole subdivision. Judith went into a tailspin that took a day to recover her bearings.

Before that the quest for someone to tell them how to proceed and all their quests fizzling and with each quest they became stronger until eventually they did everything themselves as far as instigating and making decisions.

UTOPIA, BEAUTY, ARTISTRY were the guiding drives for both Judith and John. Both in different ways and different timing could get their feet on the ground and let reality break through. Judith was more inclined to tough it out, stay with it. That was the farm in her background whereas John had an elite urban background. So strong was Judith's self reliance that to depend upon others was unsettling to her. They more often could not see as clearly as she with her intuition the possibilities of a venture. The ones who did rely upon themselves were not as tangled up in *UTOPIA, BEAUTY, ARTISTRY* as she. Judith had often to rid herself of these three drives before she could get down to brass tacks. And that endeavor often saddened her. Why can't people see what I see? Why can't people be perfect? she would ask herself, hurt and alone.

So it was natural and easy for John and Judith to explore Selene Mountain and begin to plan for powerful and beautiful places on earth available to all classes—the young, the old, the middle, the worker, the venturer. All who loved beauty and a beautiful way of life.

They planned for themselves while sitting on ledges, boulders, under pines, eating salted peanuts which they shelled and let the ground have the shells. Judith and John had things to tell, things to do which were too unique to fit within a usual job setting. Somehow, somewhere there must be a way to supplement incomes and ease out of occupations which limited them. There was more to giving than religious tithing, they often acknowledged to each other. Before the venture of Selene Mountain was over, the strongest pull for their gifts were to the persons who came at the right time to give them answers and the encouragement they needed. They were not in the venture to build themselves a personal empire but to do something from which life would be better.

But any definite meaning to the powerful dream would not come.

"I'll pray for you," Alma said, "and you for me."

"I will," Judith assured Alma and herself.

"I have a feeling Dennis will earn $50,000 next year. And to follow that Medina Homes wants him. There is always great possibility."

"I wish cutting out some of this nonsense of Burbank's was easier," Judith said.

"The citizen hasn't anyone helping. You don't get the truth from the media. The schools are way off. The politicians are afraid to lead," Dennis told them.

"You're right!" Jarvis said. "Did you go to hear Burbank?"

"Yes, we did," John answered.

"What did you think of his speech?"

"I'd like to know what he's going to do with all the water on Federal land? Is he going to store it? He's against dams!" Judith asked.

Jarvis answered her. "He intends to sell it out of state."

Dennis said, "Closer to home for us is rescinding logging contracts."

"I think the courts will throw that out. The forests are in bad condition. They're tinder boxes. This business of fires are nature's way of cleaning the forests is dangerous talk," Jarvis said with finality.

Joyce announced she wanted to call it quits for the evening and invited Judith and John to join them for breakfast.

"Maybe we will," John said, "If we wake as early as you."

CHAPTER 6
MS. ALENE CARVER'S STUDENTS

Ms. Carver put more environmental posters with their alarming information, but soothed by the comfort of the natural wild, on the school room display wall. The environmental material was free and it kept coming. The textbooks were full of it too. The new Educational Environmental Act now required a certain amount of time and space to be allotted to the enviroment, its needs, its problems and solutions, and reports of dissemination of this information was required to be sent to the administration to be turned in to the Western States Environmental Congress, a non-governmental organization.

Ms. Carver grew up on a ranch near Luna City. Her childhood was spent on camping trips into the mountains herding sheep or cattle, with members of her family. For a time they lived right in the valley with high peaks encircling them. Horses were second nature to her. She had spent considerable time riding for pleasure. Strenuous backpacking she didn't do because there was no need for this extra strenuous exercise. There was plenty of work-exercise on the ranch.

She often wished the sheep and cattle people would send some of these beautiful posters to tell what their experiences in this beautiful area were. But sadly she knew these people to be independent, self-reliant, and lacking time and money for such an endeavor as to match all these wonderful posters. Ranchers worked long hours. Some in the family held a town job out of necessity.

Compared to Ms. Carver's childhood in the West, many of her students had lived lives deprived of the wildness of nature. Pavements, noise, traffic, buildings so tall they only saw a part of the sky at a time. They had moved to Luna City with their parents and siblings from far away cities and they were intensely concerned about saving Planet Earth. These were not city housing project children living nightly with gunfire, nor door key children. They knew nothing of the Western Ranch. Ms. Carver had tried to describe ranching and farm life but it was of no avail to her or to her students. One day she got the bright idea of taking her students to a ranch and letting them experience life there for one half day. If it worked, they could do it often.

With the walls full of birds, eagles, animals—grizzlies, elk, deer, coyotes—endangered free flowing rivers, bad dams, backpackers, campers, rafters, kayakers, Ms. Carver asked her 4th graders, "How would you like to visit a ranch for half a day?"

The suggestion was met with a show of hands.

Ms. Carver had been yearning to take them and in the back of her mind she had thought of Matt and Ida Stahlek. The Stahleks were good people, always ready to lend a hand to help the community.

"I think I know of a ranch we could visit. But I'll have to ask. In the meantime we might think of what we'd like to share with the ranch. You know, what we're doing for Planet Earth because I know ranchers do a lot."

"We could show them our recycling projects."

Excitement grew. "Ooooh! I'd be scared if we saw a bear!" Eunice Easterly spoke cautiously.

"Yeah! Or a mountain lion!" Losso Damuel cried enthusedly.

"Now listen! We're not going to the Moctezuma National Forest! We're going to a ranch where people live! Like you and me! You might see chickens and farm animals but you're not going to see wild animals!"

The visit was set. Ms. Carver's 4th Graders would visit Ida Stahlek at her ranch. The Stahleks, Matt and Ida, neighbored and lent a hand to others. They participated in their church, in the Grange, in the Farm Bureau. Their children in 4-H. It was natural for Ida Stahlek to greet the idea of Ms. Carver and her 4th Graders visiting her at the ranch. Twenty years ago, or maybe even ten, the visit of the school children to the Stahlek ranch may not have needed to occur. Then there would not have been so many families from far away moved to Luna City.

The Stahleks lifestyle was greatly different from most of Ms. Carver's 4th Graders except the two or three local old timers' children—Martha Stahlek, the granddaughter of Ida, and Johnny Sandstrom, the grandson of John and Judith Sandstrom who knew a lot about mountains from his grandparents' venture into developing *Quiet Mountain* homesites on Selene Mountain. Bobby Cameron was a new student but he seemed more like an old timer's family because he and his family had melted into the community so well. But Losso Damuel's family were of a very different background from the East and from the world of finance. Eunice Easterly had her somewhat famous brother, Egbert, who got into all the environmental protests and whom Eunice often complained about in school.

It was this difference that Ms. Carver wished her 4th Graders to see. Ida Stahlek was a saver beyond anything these 4th graders could imagine even though they were very taken with the idea of recycling.

Mrs. Stahlek saved string. Any length of it. She had it in balls of different colors. String for emergencies, or for when anyone wanted string, to save a trip to town to buy a piece of string. She saved aluminum foil. She smoothed it out, folded it in squares and re-used it. She saved scraps of material from clothes she made. Often they went into quilts, or were given away to other friends to make their quilts. She saved paper sacks. They were good to carry garden vegetables in. When the town was young and Mrs. Stahlek was young, she was sent to town to sell the fresh garden vegetables for her own money. Sacks were always handy. She saved all old garments and cut them into strips for making rag rugs. At one time her living room and bedroom floors were covered wall to wall with woven rag rugs.

Today's nation's trash engulfed her. Where did it all come from? It was hard to comprehend that people have to be trained to save. It seemed sinful, unappreciative of God's bounty to throw away so much. Aren't people even thankful anymore? What's to become of us?

Matt Stahlek also saved. He saved binder twine, wire, rope chains, scraps of lumber, screening. He made much of his machinery work with the spare parts on hand. Sometimes he reused parts for other purposes.

The 4th graders arrived at the Stahlek ranch with the newspaper "Mini Page" anxious to tell Mrs. Stahlek what they were doing to save Planet Earth and to find out how she and people like her have fared so well for so long. The young students had chosen some award-winning projects: Recycling, Water Conservation, Nature for All. The van parked in the back yard. The students caught a glimpse of chickens. They headed for them begging to be allowed to play with them.

The chickens were feeding in a small pen with very high fencing. Mrs. Stahlek could see the disappointment on the children's faces and the dismay on Ms. Carver's. Ms. Carver took control and announced, "We've been studying a little about range chickens. Maybe it's a good time for you to tell us more."

"My idea of *range* does not apply to chickens in a farm yard."

"They think *range* must be special because they pay so much more for them."

"Yeah, my dad says they hold us up!" said Losso Damuel.

"We have friends who have chickens and we buy our eggs from them," said Bobby Cameron.

"Yeah, but your chickens lay eggs and these don't!" Losso said.

"Yes, these lay eggs," Ida Stahlek said.

"Where do the eggs we buy in the store come from?" Eunice Easterly asked.

"From chickens! Like these!"

"Do *range* chickens lay eggs too?" Losso asked.

"Yes!"

"*Range* chicken is a modern term, don't you think?" Ms. Carver said. "Around the city you have such large chicken farms and the chickens are given many substances to make them grow fast and produce more eggs. They do not roam freely and so your parents have learned to distinguish them from these chickens who are not penned up and fed hormones to make them grow and produce."

"Can *range* chickens have little chickens like the chickens in the stores?" Eunice asked.

Ida was amazed. She had never thought of these questions. Then a smile came over her face. "Why, of course, they lay eggs, the eggs hatch, and chickens come out! Where else would they come from?" Ida walked closer to the pen. "These chickens are large. They're called White Rocks because they are large and they lay so much. Their eggs are large and very white."

Ms. Carver felt her fourth graders needed an explanation. "What do you mean 'they lay so much'"?

"Yeah," Losso said. "Are they awake all day?"

"I mean they lay so many eggs. We speak of 'laying hens.'

"The chickens don't have much room! We wanted to play with them. But the fence is too high," Eunice complained.

Ida choked on this. "I'd rather see them out in the barnyard scratching for food. They need the exercise."

"We want to play with them."

"See over there right under that dying pinon? He's not moving now. He's watching us. Can you see the coyote? There! He moved! He's casing my chickens."

"I see him!" Johnny Sandstrom said as he pulled Bobby Cameron's head down. "See right back of that sage brush. There! He's moving."

"I see him Grandma," Martha Stahlek said.

A student started toward the coyote. "Let's make a pet of him!"

Another student followed. "I want to pet him too."

Ms. Carver said, "No. Let the coyote be. Come back!"

Eunice said, "My mother thinks coyotes are pretty. She thinks it's a shame we don't have more so we children can watch them and know what they are. She thinks we've lost a lot of animals on this planet."

Mrs. Stahlek swallowed hard. "My chickens used to run all over our yard and hunt food all day long. But now we have to keep them fenced and watch them besides. Coyotes want to eat them too. I could let the chickens out but we'll have to watch each and everyone of them. We'll get them back in the fence with food. Although they've just been fed," she added warily.

Ms. Carver said, "Oh I wouldn't bother, Mrs. Stahlek. We can come again when they've not been fed. How long will that coyote hang around?"

"Until it's removed."

"What do you mean?"

"We call the wildlife people and they come and capture him and take him away."

"Are you going to call Wildlife?"

"I'll have to as soon as I can. Mr. Stahlek is putting up hay. Sometimes it takes two of us just to watch the chickens and then we have the cattle and young calves too. With a coyote stalking we can't turn our backs."

"Go call them and we'll watch. Will the coyote bother with us watching?"

"I don't think so but they're becoming more bold all the time."

Mrs. Stahlek went into her house. The coyote moved stealthily into full view of the students. He stood like a show dog—front legs slightly forward, back legs at ease, the bushy tail resting over the right hind leg like a woman's luxurious stole over her shoulder, ears pointing back and alert, with face turned slightly right, eyeing the students, the eyes reflecting thought, a master and surveyor of the range. He eyed chickens in a pen. He looked full but he may have others that need a chicken dinner that can be picked up and carried home.

The students wanted to pet the coyote. Some started in its direction. Ms. Carver said, "Wait! I'll get the camera. We'll take a picture of him. Don't disturb him. Maybe we can get a picture."

Mrs. Stahlek came back to the students. Ms. Carver asked if they shouldn't wait until the man came for the coyote.

"Oh, no! He has to come from Red Rocks over east of here and he was out on a call. I could only leave a message."

"What will you do until he gets here?"

"I'll have to watch them. I had other things to do but I'll have to wait."

"At night?"

"We put them in the chicken shed. We've had to coyote proof it. They've torn a lot of the tar paper loose trying to get in anyway. We'll have to pray tonight."

Mrs. Stahlek wished Matt could shoot the coyote. That's what the Wildlife will do anyway but now you have to go by regulations and take your chances.

Ms. Carver said since the coyote is here, I believe we should come again and show our recycling and have you tell us this angle of life on a ranch.

"Perhaps so," Mrs. Stahlek agreed. "Perhaps next week after the coyote is removed would be better."

CHAPTER 7

ROBERT MARKHAM, THE FILM PRODUCER

The phone was ringing when Judith entered her office. "J and J Development Company, Judith Sandstrom speaking."

"Robert Markham. I'm in town looking for mountain property. I'd like to be shown Quiet Mountain if someone can work me in tomorrow."

"I can do it. When can you go up?"

"Nine tomorrow."

"Come to my office and I'll take you up."

Robert Markham arrived camera around his neck. "I'd like to take pictures. Want them with me in California. I'm looking for a second home. Somewhere quiet. A retreat away from my work. I produce documentaries. I was up there when the sheriff's car came up the hill."

95

Judith acknowledged with a nod. A shock of unruly light brown hair fell over Markham's forehead.

"Quiet Mountain land is beautiful!" Judith said.

They rode in Judith's jeep following the canyon rim with Beaver Creek below them.

"I have a habit of snapping pictures wherever I go. I took pictures of the sheriff and your realtor and the demolished sign. I developed them. You may have them." He pulled them out of his slender briefcase and placed them between the bucket seats.

"That's good of you. Thank you."

Judith drove all the way up to the jeep trail below the upper tank where she parked her jeep when Elmer Jarvis and the young bulldozer operator were working on the water line. Markham enjoyed each panoramic view—the newly mowed meadow, rimmed by mountains to the north and to the south and the gracious snow peaks to the west, eight miles distant as the hawk flies—the whole valley fell away before him.

Markham turned in his seat to seek at every turn, through the dazzling sunlight on the pine needles, a view of the peaks, snow covered, glistening, and to breathe in the spirit which accompanied them.

"Can you hear the creek up this high?"

"In the spring you can. When it's rushing. You can also hear the water falls coming down from the mountains all around you. I like the wind in the pines too," Judith said.

"You could do a lot with these boulders," Markham said.

"They have been used. Everything can be left in its natural state—wild and wooded."

"I read that glowing feature of Quiet Mountain in Sunday's paper. So I drove up to see for myself. It's better than I ever could have imagined."

They walked over a lot Markham had looked at yesterday. He turned and looked across the valley at the snow peaks again.

"I'd like to know what your thoughts were the first time you saw this view? I wonder if it's anything like I'm feeling right now? And yesterday."

Judith looked at Markham. His eyes were blue, almost as blue as the steel-blue eyes of Damuel. But Markham's eyes reflected a curious search for new experience. They were not fixed in a tunnel. They were eyes that invite you to explore with them. Eyes with a glint of merriment.

Judith thought she knew what Markham's feeling was, but it's too much to reveal in an instant. "I wrote about my feelings and we used the copy with slides we put together, with one of our buyers, for sales presentations. But we refrained from using the slides. There was so much opposition to development in general. I'll give you a copy when we return to the office."

Markham looked again at the plat. "Do you think there is a lot I'd like better than this? Should I look at more?"

"You can have much privacy on this lot. It's large. There's this flattish place in the center and the boulders guarding it in back. You can choose to overlook all the stuff that some day might happen in the valley and look directly at the peaks. Or you can view the valley. You have a choice Also to the north end of the lot you have a tremendous view of everything. Keep the wildness. See that snag with the holes left from the fallen limbs? Georgia O'Keeffe paints them and the sky through them and you have one right there!" Judith pointed to it. "Keep it and let the woodpeckers have a tree too."

"I love it!" he said. "It's what I need— nature. Let me examine it one more day. I'll stay over and I'll get back in touch." He opened his briefcase and pulled out a business card, wrote his room number at the Grand Hotel on the back. "You can reach me here," he said.

Judith took the card and slowly studied Markham. "Were you taking pictures of the miner at Burbank's speech?"

"Yes, I got some good pictures of him."

"Did you write some of his conversation? His vows?"

"I didn't need to! They were so strong in the face of Burbank! But I intend to. His defiance is what attracted me!"

"Yes!"

CHAPTER 8
RAFTERS AND THE CITY

The Washtub Rafting Company used the city
riverfront park area for loading and unloading
passengers. They had an agreement with the
City Park and Recreation Department dating
back eleven years. They were not the first.
In the decade since, many more rafting
companies had begun using public park areas
along the Luna River as it wound its way
through the city. This increased use of city
parks plus all other increased uses caused the
city to look again at the commercial nature of
rafting. The Council sent notice to all the
rafting companies to make other arrangements
for the next summer. Next summer city will
require a special permit, a fee, and
conditions to be met for parking, and other
uses of the riverfront areas.

The rafting companies argue their case and present their excuses. "We keep customers out of the congested downtown area during busy summer tourist months."

"We are a safety net for people in trouble on the river."

The city manager of course reminded the rafters that they were the people on the river.

Washtub's owner believed she was operating raft trips in compliance with the city's Riverfront Plan.

The question is, the city manager stated, whether or not the city can allow commercial operations on the sites. Then he also stated concerns: congestion on the river and heavy use of loading and unloading areas by the rafters at four different public park sites—

the river banks to the north, west, and south plus the City Park close to the downtown area.

There were so many pleas and arguments that the city council set a date for all the rafting companies to meet at city hall to review the problem and work toward a solution. Wilson, city councilman, told the rafters that the city was not in the business of controlling the competitive market but would work with them in ensuring fairness. "We just provide a level playing field."

The rafters saw the handwriting on the wall because other marketers had been denied the free use of city streets. So they slowly moved out of the public park areas on down the river and became squatters on private lands. Washtubs latched onto Stahlek's land and they didn't want cattle in the way of their clients getting into or out of the rafts. They made their claims to Matt Stahlek. "We are the dominant use!"

Stahlek looked at his herd of cattle and couldn't buy it since his deed was to the center of the river. But following his accustomed habit of helping his neighbor he told them he would try to accommodate them if they're not at the river bank during the watering time for his cattle mornings and evenings.

For a while it was workable. But as rafting became more popular more companies came into existence. Now there were eight companies using Matt Stahlek's watering bank. Matt knew he had a problem and would search for a way to handle it.

In the meantime, Ms. Carver asked Ida Stahlek if she had a picture of Arthur's sheep which she could put on the classroom wall so the students could see what a band of sheep looked like. "Well, yes, I do have. That Robert Markham has been out photographing them as Arthur and his men were enroute with them from New Mexico. I have an enlarged photo. They're so white and pretty. Just before lambing and shearing. That Markham is an excellent photographer."

Ida found the 14 x 16 colored shot of Arthur's 1,000 band of sheep coming up from the sage brush of New Mexico. Alene Carver was amazed at the beauty of the picture. She quickly gave it the title: "A River of Sheep". Arthur was in front of the band with a working branch with many limbs in his left hand. The sheep were full and rounded and the river stretched diagonally across the photo with a switch back of the river of sheep beyond the county dirt road just below the pinon and pine. The green, the sage, the brown dirt, the white sheep made a striking scene. Ida offered to get it framed if Ms. Carver thought it important.

As Ida continued the preparation for the students' visit, she drifted back into when she was young remembering her mother cleaning out the insides of the entrails of hogs and restuffing them with sausage. She washed the entrails in a large tub-pan, turning them inside out, cleaning all of the crevices. At the finish they were rinsed with boiling water and then stuffed. Mrs. Stahlek washed her younger brother's diapers by hand and afterwards was rewarded with her mother's hand lotion. Later she washed her own menstrual cloths by hand. She remembered fondly the first isinglass snap-on windows for roadsters and touring cars and the first steering wheels made of cereal instead of metal. She didn't think she could tell her memories to the young children. And that was why she was remembering. The paper was full of the greed of ranchers, especially the letters to the editor by the newcomers. Sometimes she felt her saving was considered greed and hoarding by the modern generation. Their throw-aways were considered correct disdain for an evil economic system.

It was planned on this visit the students would bring their Recycling Project Book and Ida was to show her recycling as a common interest so she was collecting things to be handy for the visit.

The van arrived and the students hopped out the sliding door. Ms. Carver stepped down from the driver's seat. "They've just finished a project and want to show you their work book."

Eunice Easterly asked immediately, "What happened to the coyote? Did you get another?"

Mrs. Stahlek said, "No the chickens didn't want another coyote. The Wildlife man took it to a new home where there are no little chicks and chickens."

But Eunice still worried. "What will the coyote eat now?"

Mrs. Stahlek was fighting feeling overwhelmed. "He'll find other wild life to eat in the natural wild."

Ms. Carver helped out. "He'll be more happy in the wild with other wild creatures. He is wild and the chickens are domestic. Like your kitty cat and your dog. Understand?"

"I haven't fed the chickens. We can play with them first or see the scrap book. The students may decide."

"I believe the scrapbook would be the first order," Ms. Carver said.

"Then let's go inside."

Mrs. Stahlek led them to her living room. Her uneasiness stayed with her. She could not get rid of it. Her old carpet was threadbare. She spoke to Ms. Carver. "In the good times of the Sixties and Seventies I would have had new carpet laid. I've thought of taking up this threadbare one and restoring the ranch house to its wooden floor. But I think this is better than bare wood floors in the winter."

Her eyes glazed over as she remembered the soft feel of the plush carpet when they laid it in the early Seventies. How warm it was in the winter! She spoke her thoughts again to Ms. Carver. "This carpet was laid in the early Seventies. My husband, Matt, was once wealthy but now nearly bankrupt. It is because of so many regulations which take away our rights granted to us by the Constitution."

Ms. Carver reached her hand out and patted Mrs. Stahlek's arm. Mrs. Stahlek, almost on the verge of tears, gathered herself together. "All right, let's see the recycling book. I'm a saver myself."

Johnny Sandstrom opened the book to a snapshot. "Here's how our Waste Watchers have saved reusable cups and lunch bags."

Bobby Cameron turned the page. "And we reuse cardboard boxes for our storage in our classroom."

Losso Damuel turned another page. "And we've gone to the school basement where they have bins of paper with writing on only one side. Now we're using the other side."

Mrs. Stahlek said, "That's very good. That's how we do it on the ranch."

"And we collect newspapers! Do you have newspapers for us to pick up? We'll take them for you."

"I'm afraid I don't. You see we use them all up on the ranch."

"Some days at school are paperless days," Ms. Carver directed. "Who wants to tell Mrs. Stahlek about water conservation? What does conservation mean?"

"It means save it."

"Use it only when you need it."

"Don't waste it."

Ms. Carver asked, "Is this inside the house or outside?"

"Both!" the students answered.

Ms. Carver kept directing. "How do you water the lawn using conservation?"

"Water it in the evening when the hot sun doesn't evaporate it," a student answered.

Losso Damuel asked, "How do you conserve your water, Mrs. Stahlek?"

Mrs. Stahlek felt more and more in another time, another world. "We don't have water for our lawns. There is a good spring that this whole area draws drinking water from. When you leave you'll see the water tank on my husband's truck. He fills it and we use it for household purposes and for bathing and for laundry."

Mrs. Stahlek spoke to Ms. Carver: "Matt and I, with others, have worked so hard for the dam. It's been thirty years since the government approved it. We waited through wars and environmental impact studies and now endangered species that the government had just painstakingly eliminated for the trout. It's never ending." She sighed and cursed herself for having to tell such a hopeless, useless story.

Losso said, "My mother says dams are bad and we don't need them."

Ms. Carver's face tensed. "Perhaps your mother has not had to live without running water as Mrs. Stahlek has. Has your mother ever hauled water for your bath?"

"No." Losso giggled. "She just fills the tub full."

Ms. Carver told Losso, "Tell your mother Mrs. Stahlek hauls her bath and drinking water." Then Ms. Carver redirected the visit. "Show Mrs. Stahlek what you've learned of where water comes from."

The students answered until they'd covered all sources.

"It comes from the ground, rain, streams, rivers, lakes, oceans."

Eunice asked, "Why doesn't Mrs. Stahlek get a well?"

Mrs. Stahlek answered. "In this area the ground is not charged with water."

Losso asked, "What does she mean, 'charged with water'"?

Ms. Carver instructed, "She means there's no source to put water in the ground. The mesa is much higher than the river."

Losso studied Mrs. Stahlek as if he didn't know what to make of a person living with no water. "How do your chickens get water?" he asked skeptically.

Mr. Stahlek puts water in their drinking pans from the water he hauls."

"But why did you want to live here if you knew there was no water?" Losso asked.

"There was water when we came here but now New Mexico, the state to the south, claims it."

Ms. Carver explained, "That is what the dam is supposed to do—furnish water for both states, Colorado and New Mexico, and for the Indians, and for the water that your mother and all the rest of us are using and may in some drought period run out of."

"Oh," Losso said, a little more politely.

"What about the coyote?" Eunice asked.

"The coyote goes to the river down below."

Another student tired of the worrying, asked, "What do you recycle, Mrs. Stahlek?"

"Lots and lots of things. Like your class we recycle paper and write on the clean side, and reuse cups, plates, tin foil. I smooth the tin foil out, fold it in squares and re-use and re-use it."

Mrs. Stahlek walked to a cupboard in the kitchen. She pulled out a file folder from among her cookbooks and opened the folder. Returning to the living room she said, "Here is a bunch of it. I always feel future generations, like you youngsters and your children and their children will need all the things we use. I feel responsible for them. I have no idea if bauxite is limited or not."

Ms. Carver instructed, "Bauxite is what aluminum is made from. Miners mine it out of the ground and it becomes aluminum."

Ms. Carver addressed Mrs. Stahlek: "I'll bet you recycle much more than you've told us."

Mrs. Stahlek admitted, "Oh I save string. Balls of it for emergencies, or for anyone wanting string, to save a trip to town to buy a piece of string. Now I'm saving them in balls of different colors. Come, I'll show you the bin where I keep them." It also was in the kitchen. "This green garden string for plants. This is strong nylon. This is packing string for sending parcels. This is heavier yellow cord. It's fun to save. What do you save at home? In your own room?"

A boy answered. "Baseball cards. I have a good collection. My Dad says I have some that are worth a lot."

"That's wonderful. Do you like to show them to your friends?"

"Yes. We meet and compare and sometimes trade cards."

"I think most people like to save something," Mrs. Stahlek said. "What I do with friends is save scraps of material from clothes I've made. Most of the time we put them into quilts. Or I give them to friends who are making quilts and need a particular piece or a particular color. It's fun to meet with eight or ten women and stitch a quilt. Have you ever seen women stitch a quilt together?"

Ms. Carver described it further. "They stretch the quilt in a large frame as large as the quilt. The men make the frames and they fill a room this size. That's why eight or ten get around the quilt in chairs and stitch the quilt. They stitch the top to the soft middle padding and on through the back of the quilt."

"It's fun to meet your neighbors at a quilting bee. We call them quilting bees because we're all busy as bees," Mrs. Stahlek told the students. "We want to get the quilt done and out of the center of the room."

119

Now the visit was over and time for the students to climb back into Ms. Carver's van and for Mrs. Stahlek to start supper.

First, she fed the chickens and scanned for coyotes. Matt arrived later than usual. He was a powerfully built man but beyond his prime with not the physical strength he used to have. Arthur, their son, is the physically powerful one now. But looking at Matt one can still see all the strength there was. He had in his hands two large branding irons of about 18 inches in height.

"Someone is rustling cattle," he said. "Sullivan and Tuttle that I know of are missing cattle. We think someone's testing the water!"

Ida studied Matt and thought 'one more thing!'

"I brought these irons in from the shed. I just feel they're safer out of reach." He hid the irons in the pantry.

"The sheriff is working on the problem. There's not a trace of the cattle. They've not been butchered. No parts. Just missing. When I watered the cattle there were six rafts of tourists in the river. I had to wait for them, herding the cattle away from the bank. Dobbin did a good job and so did Collie. We waited quite a while for them to pack their gear and leave the water."

CHAPTER 9

FRANKEL, THE MONKEYWRENCHER

There were preliminary meetings the day before Frankel's public address in the evening in the Fine Arts Auditorium of the Anglo/Indian College. Tom Gerry, who accompanied Fred Frankel, met with students at the Student Union with plenty of beer on ice. Tom thrilled the students telling how the Monkeywrenchers came into being. It was the first real thing in his life that gave him purpose and direction. An army brat, he joined the Marines and it was a total disaster. He couldn't take an order, any order. He spent his time in solitary and the brig until he received an undesirable discharge. He was then attracted to Barry Goldwater and joined the Republican Party. Through Goldwater he studied Jeffersonian democracy. Finally he found the counter culture and went from supporting George Wallace to supporting Eldridge Cleaver. He did drugs. Let his hair grow long and went to rock-and-roll concerts. Spent a lot of time in prison. At the end of the Viet Nam war he was confused and at loose ends. Demonstrations had shrunk from 30,000 to 75. He was thinking of settling down and getting a job when a friend suggested he hike the Rockies. That did it. He discovered he loved wild country and needed it. Eventually he met his first environmentalist and began reading the holy book, *The Monkey wrench Gang* by Edward Abbey.

He immediately went out and cut down about 90 percent of the billboards in Jefferson county. Then he met Fred Frankel.

"I now work three days a month to pay rent and utilities, another two days earn me spending change. Those five days of labor, augmented by food stamps provide the necessities, and the rest of the month I'm free to roam about and cause trouble. It's fun! It's great! Hardly a day goes by that we don't do an action against industrialized society.

"We met, Fred and I, and Morris on a hike, hunting for a peak to climb in the Sonoran Desert. We had no maps and didn't know exactly where this peak was. Just heard it was a good climb. It was a two-week trip. We were driving all over the place just for fun hunting this volcano to climb. Driving around on dirt roads. When we couldn't drive any further we parked the van and walked.

"Anyway we were drinkin' beer and having these incredibly exciting, energetic conversations. We knew by this time we had to get more radical. Take a more radical approach if we were ever going to achieve any goals.

"We drank and talked. We built up a lot of solidarity on this trip. The moment actually happened after we started home in the van that we decided to start a new group. I remember drawing up the logo while we were bumping along in the van. We still have a copy of the first drawing and the lines are real squiggly from the dirt road. Hughey and Fred and Morris started screamin' out all the things that were going to be in our platform and we scribbled those things down. By the time we got home we had started *Mother Green!* We had a manifesto, a name and a logo.

"We had this notion that *Mother Green!* would always be a tribe. It seemed romantic. Now I begin to see the truth in it. We would not be an organization. We'd have no formal leaders, no board of directors, no hierarchy. We would be a tribe. We invented our own tribal language.

"Our goal is not to save remaining wilderness but to save all of it, and recreate vast areas of wilderness in areas now developed! *Mother Green!* did not simply oppose new dams, it demanded the dismantling of old ones. The four you have here in this area need to be dismantled. *Mother Green!* promises never to compromise.

"*Mother Green!* would employ direct action. We'd advocate ecotage or monkeywrenching in defense of the ecosystem. There are many helpful suggestions. Here's a book that gives many ways to commit ecotage.

"Fred got burned out on Rare II. Seven years of seventy hours a week. Between speeches, he's a rabble rouser. He needs calm. That's why I'm here with him."

The evening came and Frankel walked out on the stage in the big Fine Arts Auditorium in army camouflage and a dull brown stocking cap. He shied away from the microphone which he didn't like. He spoke in a raspy voice from overuse. It was hard to hear him. He raised his voice higher and asked if the crowd could hear him now.

"Yeah!" he crowd roared. "Yippy Yahoo!"

Frankel started out in a slow andante, a soft sell. "We need humility," he said dispassionately like the quiet of the wilderness itself. "We need to listen to the forest. Listen to the quiet. We need to become the wilderness in defense of itself."

It seemed the wilderness was speaking itself to the crowd.

"Yeah!" the crowd affirmed him.

"Think what it must have been like a mere forty years ago when the grizzlies roamed these mountains unmolested by man! A mother with her grizzly cubs foraging for berries, drinking from pure Rocky Mountain sparkling spring water. And the peregrine falcon soaring overhead, plunging straight down at speeds of 200 miles per hour to catch its prey in flight! And the bald eagles flying in pairs leaving a shadow on that far mountain! The coyote, cunning, adaptable, except to poison bait. The praying, nibbling prairie dog out from its subterranean tunnel! The bony chub and the razorback sucker, a civilization in the water almost lost! This wilderness had it all once! What's happened to it?"

Frankel's fist was in the air. His eyes were almost closed. Mouth wide open, white teeth showing, framed by his mustache and beard. The roar of the crowd had a life of its own. He pitched his voice higher, it cracking and thin from overuse. His face reddened with strain.

"Biocentrism! Not anthropocentrism! We need biocentrism! *You* are going to decide if there will be wolves, grizzlies, eagles, falcons, coyotes, old-growth forests in the West. It's *you, your* generation on this march today."

He paused again while the crowd reacted with renewed energy. He was getting the crowd entirely with him. There was a rising bedlam of whoops and yips.

"What's wrong?" he asked. "People and resources! That's where it all began. Unless we take the message to the people and keep taking it to them, we are going to lose everything that's precious and beautiful in this world. So let's go and tell the Forest Service, the government, that we don't want roads, we don't want clear-cuts. We want *forests!* We want *wilderness!* We want the powerful grizzly, the loping coyote, the lightning falcon, the bony chub. We don't want eroded streams. We don't want roads gouging out all that's beautiful and green on this planet. We want to be alive as part of the earth." Frankel ended with his fist stretched to the rafters and the crowd was transformed with Frankel's energy.

"He moved me," Stan said and there were tears in his red eyes and his voice had caught. "We need to do something" he said to relieve the pressure inside himself.

"Yeah!" Egbert said. "Let's go to the reception and see if we can talk with him. I need to calm down!"

A copy of *The Monkeywrench Gang* was thrust into Stan's hands at the reception. They did not get to face Frankel one on one. Frankel left early to rest before his speech on the circuit the next night. They returned downtown and by accident they stopped by the candle shop. Egbert knew about Cecelia's candles because they were on every table of the five-star resort where his parents have a membership. Through the plate glass window they could see that Cecelia had a customer. They exchanged knowing glances. They could involve the customer too. Spread the word. Maybe get a new convert. Paraffin is bad. Oil is bad. The customer is guilty of using a petrol product just as Cecelia is guilty of making candles out of paraffin. They knew if they had found a bigger civil disobedience to do they could earn $12.00 @ hour and belong to a congress, a federation, a bureau—something with the sound of government.

Cecelia's candle flowers were more beautiful than true life forms. She had just finished decorating pale, translucent faintly orchid sticks with flowers. A white lily with pale yellow stamen driving right up the fully opened flower, supported and guarded by dark forest green leaves and stem. The sunlight shining through the translucent pale pastels was ethereal. There was the purple/blue columbine. The shop was full of candles with all kinds of flowers ready for shipping.

Cecelia, a dark brunette with very fair complexion, wore her hair in several pony tail braids. She would be going out after closing shop and wore a white cocktail dress with black piping and trim. Girlish. She had two fatherless children to support. Candles were lovely, safe and repetitive.

The spruce tree three were dressed cutlandishly, properly for their roles of political activism. They entered the shop. They felt high. They could accomplish anything!

Cecelia, still busy with her customer, glanced warily at them. Egbert caught her glance. "How long does it take you to make one of these candles?"

Cecelia looked puzzled. Are they wanting her to teach them? "I give classes in candlemaking," she offered and tried to resume the care of the customer. The interrogators ignored her answer.

"What do you use to make your candles?"

Cecelia hesitated.

"What material?" they zeroed in.

"Different kinds?"

"What is this one made of?" The interrogator took the candle from the customer and held it in front of Cecelia, holding her with his gaze.

"Paraffin."

"Paraffin! God! she uses paraffin! She plays right along with the petroleum industry."

"Then you support the oil and gas drilling going on in this area!"

Cecelia looked scared. She looked cautiously at her customer. Her eyes pled for help.

"You make a lot of profit on oil and gas drilling?"

"I'm not into oil and gas drilling," Cecelia said very clearly.

"But you do make money from it!"

"Not really."

"Not really! You do all this work without money?"

Cecelia did not answer.

"Maybe you should just quit then."

"Maybe she doesn't have a planning permit. This is a dangerous manufacture. She could set the whole block on fire."

"Yeah, bet the Planning Department doesn't even know she exists."

The protestors walked around the shop handling fragile candles. Cecelia wished they would leave.

"Why doesn't she use beeswax, a natural product?"

"It's not available," Cecelia explained weakly, keeping an eye on each candle, hoping they do not break the candles she was ready to ship. She had a deadline. Customers were waiting to be served. She could tell the customers knew something was going on but they were patient as if to help as much as they could.

"You'd better find beeswax. Paraffin is a finite source. It'll be depleted within seven years."

Cecelia had never been confronted before on her activity of candlemaking. The effect upon her was to investigate beeswax. She learned it is harder to come by and she would have to raise the price of her candles. She lived in nameless fear. Without realizing it she had given sanction to her tormentors, became willing to bear any injustice if she could be let alone, sacrifice her own interests and pursuit of happiness, concede them moral validity to their claims and assume her guilt in the petroleum and gas wars, if she could be let alone. That day she lost her business innocence. It never would be the same.

And for Stan, Egbert and the other tree cutters, Burbank was coming to town again. The Home Secretary would be speaking at the college on his way back to D.C. from Wyoming. To hear Burbank was a must.

CHAPTER 10
PERMANENT RESTRAINING ORDER

The postman delivered J & J's restraining order. Darth Damuel signed the return receipt. He then stepped inside his study and picked up his long silver and turquoise Indian crafted letter opener to read the order. A malignant smile rested on his face. He filed the order in the file cabinet under "Q". Then he walked up the mountain to see how the development was going. He saw the pine pushed over and could ascertain the direction of the work to be done. He decided to shift his action to protest the pine being pushed over. With this action it might be easier to get the homeowners involved on his side. He stopped at each home on the walk down and began his inflammatory exaggerations.

"They're making a mess of the mountain! They're clearcutting! There won't be a tree left!"

As he walked down his speeches became more wildly exaggerated.

"Damage is already done to our home values! The least we can do now is stop them! We let this get away from us!"

The homeowners were left in a state of excitement.

At noon next day Damuel took a younger homeowner, Bill Watson, with him up to the water line trenching. Jarvis took no notice of them with the attention he was giving to the young trainee. Damuel and Watson walked around the area, Damuel telling Watson what he thought would be the direction of the development of the waterline while complaining constantly of the damage being done to Mother

Earth. Watson's wife was a regular attendant of the Moctezuma Sonora Club and Damuel was making a strong impression on Watson. So strong Watson didn't really think of water.

Having Watson stirred up, Damuel suggested they call a meeting of the rest of the homeowners and get them up here to see what's going on and the damage done to their property they own down below.

With Watson's agreement to this action, Damuel walked over to Jarvis and called loudly above the noise of the cat. "Sir!"

Jarvis saw him and nodded to the trainee to shut the cat's noise down.

"Sir, I wonder if you'd mind just closing down this operation until we homeowners have a meeting and get informed on what's going on up here?" His voice had a tone of scolding to a child.

"Sir, I don't work for you. My contract is with J & J Development Company."

"Would you just wait until this evening when the homeowners can get up here to see this?"

"No, I cannot."

"Well, Sir, I don't want to get a restraining order on you but I will."

Jarvis' face took on a stifled groan like a struggle for patience. He took a deep breath and looked Damuel in the eye without blinking. Finally he said, "After Lee here quits work, I can wait a little but I cannot wait long."

"That will help a great deal," Damuel answered.

Jarvis turned back to the trainee and the cat's noise began again.

Damuel and Watson walked down the mountain calling on all homeowners they could find at home.

John Sandstrom's nose had been broken in high school football and it had never since been straight with his face.

John was a pleaser, especially with those outside his family. He was, however, endlessly patient with his and Judith's son, Johnny. John especially loved the woods. In his youth he spent many summers with his parents in Estes Park and later, as an eagle scout, the high point of his young life was in the Wisconsin Dells portaging from lake to lake. While working on his M. A. in Minnesota he'd swim alone out on Lake Johanna until he was entirely out of sight of Judith and Johnny and friends. He dearly loved Quiet Mountain and the pine, juniper and balsam, the vistas, the rim of sandstone along the valley walls.

Another of his loves was the press. He was dedicated to a free and responsible press. He had never gotten to where he could relate it to advertising. So he taught classes in journalism at the local Anglo/Indian College.

In the afternoon, after classes, he went up to Quiet Mountain to meet with Jarvis. Judith was showing property. What John saw upon arrival was quite shocking. About nine homeowners were milling and marching around the cat and the open trench, and Damuel with others chiming in from time to time, had Jarvis entirely encircled out in the open.

As John got closer to the confrontation he could hear Jarvis tell Damuel, "Sir, we are cramped for time. We need to get a full day's work in tomorrow to keep to our committed schedule."

"Well, Sir," said Damuel, "I can't run your schedule for you but I can say you weren't invited up here by any of these homeowners and we're just asking you civilly to pull out."

"I cannot do that."

"What's the matter?" John asked.

"We want whatever you're doing up here stopped," Damuel ordered.

"We can't stop," John informed him. "Bob Young needs water and road. We have commitments to all the homeowners. At this point Bob Young, a thin, lanky soul, who could buy them all out, was ambling up the trail to the confrontation scene. He usually took the route of least resistance. He was known as *Bobsy* although his name was really Robert Young. John would not like to be called *Bobsy*. John now wondered if Bobsy really wanted water. If so, he should be of help.

But John realized you could never tell which way a homeowner would go. At first Bobsy didn't want the road built to his lot because he loved the little crooked trail so much.

Damuel noticed Bob Young and hesitated in his attacks.

"If I have any holdups tomorrow, if we don't get in a full day's work, I will pull out," Jarvis said.

It seemed of no concern to Young.

"I'll have the sheriff here so that you can work," John said quietly.

"That would be fine," Jarvis acknowledged.

"We're going to have another meeting on this and we'll talk in the morning," Damuel informed.

"Don't lay a hand on this equipment," Jarvis warned before he left with John.

Milling around town, the Spruce Tree people heard that Damuel was lining up marchers to march against Judith and John cutting trees to place the upper tank and the spruce tree people decided to *warm up* on Quiet Mountain and work up to the really big Forest Service protest coming up, where they'd meet the sheriff and deputies, and chain themselves to trees and cattle guards.

Egbert and Stan arrived at Quiet Mountain as John and Jarvis were getting into their cars. Egbert and Stan did not know who had passed them, nor did John and Jarvis know which homeowners Egbert and Stan belonged to. It was no more than two ships passing silently in the night.

Egbert and Stan reached the scene of the tank excited and wanting to know what the protest was about. Damuel gave them his lowdown. "We're staying until this is settled."

"What trees will be taken?"

"I think they intend to take all of them in front of this water line they're laying," Damuel said.

"Let's take a walk," Egbert said to Stan.

They walked on up the mountain way beyond the tank. Coming back they also looked across the valley and saw the immense beauty of the place and they, too, felt the exhilaration. Their reaction was to do a CD and celebrate.

"Let's be like Fred Frankel and Tom Gerry and start our own Mother Green! group!" Egbert said.

"Yeah," Stan agreed. "No one should be living on this mountain anyway. Did you bring spikes?"

"Of course! That's what I figured we'd do!"

Next day at the noon hour while John was in class, Damuel and Watson walked up and while Lee, the novice heavy equipment operator, was sitting under a pine eating his lunch they crawled into the cab of the cat and took the keys. Lee heard the noise and looked to see Damuel jump down from the cab. He placed his sandwich in the lunch pail and ran towards Damuel and Watson. Damuel waved the keys.

"Give me those keys!"

"We're closing you down. After we decide what's to be done, we'll inform you when you can resume."

"You can't do this! It's against the law for you to take possession of what you don't own!"

"We'll see."

"I have to have those keys! I'm employed here!"

Damuel walked on indifferently.

"Don't you see? I need this job! Mr. Young needs water! Others need jobs like these!" Lee was almost crying. Then he was embarrassed to be begging like this. Damuel kept walking indifferently.

"Damn you, you mother fucker! You have no right to take the key to this cat!" Lee almost struck Damuel. He didn't know what to do to get the keys and continue his work. He turned back, got into his truck and left for Jarvis and Company.

CHAPTER 11
THE PROTEST OF TREES CUT FOR WATER LINE

Homeowners arrived at Damuel's house right after work to walk the damaged area of the downed pine and ascertain the other trees to be cut to install the water line for Bob Young and other up-the-mountain homeowners. It was like a party. Damuel pepping them, wearing a new Western hat with a fancy hat band in which was perched a good-sized feather. The homeowners made more over the feather than the hat. They wanted to know where he got a hat with such a large feather.

"I found it!" he said, "in fact, not far from here. An Indian shaman, a friend of my wife's, said it's an eagle!"

"Boy!" Siefried exclaimed.

Back at Damuel's house Greedor, Damuel's attorney, awaited them. Damuel related the events leading to the walk.

"I took the keys from the bulldozer at noon. The operator, Lee, wanted them back and I refused to release them. He left and went after his boss, Jarvis. At 2 p.m. Jarvis and Lee were at my door asking for the keys. We discussed the situation for about one and a half hours. In the beginning Jarvis was upset and abusive, including the use of foul language.

"Lee seemed to be hurting for work and by the end of the conversation, he and I were friends and we seemed to have reached an understanding.

"I gave them the right to cut or push over the trees they needed and limb them but not skid them down, nor haul them on our road, as we need to discuss this and review all our options.

"Judith was up there. I believe she was counting the trees in question.

"I asked them to please hold off until I called them with a possible solution after we meet tonight.

"They pleaded with me to please keep an eye on their equipment for them. I agreed to try but offered no responsibility for their property. Jarvis apologized numerous times for his anger and abusive language."

At this point Greedor addressed the homeowners.

"There is general destruction shared by all. There has been a gross injury. There's the possibility of a lawsuit with a large value. We need to discuss possible ways to remove the logs. Minimal damage and use biggest considerations. Perhaps having J & J Development use a chipper to get rid of fire danger."

Siefried made a motion to have loggers remove downed logs in an environmentally safe manner.

Ann Joslind requested an observer present during removal.

Damuel said, "I believe we should let them back in to work within ten days. I feel Jarvis and Lee will do their best to make all happy. We might consider a collection from the homeowners for them. They seem to be caught in the middle. This would show that we do care and want to prevent this type action again."

Most of the homeowners agreed with this suggestion. Watson agreed to moniter progress. Curtis suggested they let J & J

Development or their contractors remove the logs.

Damuel left to phone Lee and Jarvis and inform Jarvis of the homeowners' decisions.

Greedor said he would draft a letter stating homeowners provisions within ten days. He now instructed the homeowners how to capture the loss.

"Take pictures.

"Write down your feelings.

"Make recordings of the sound of the chain saw and the crash of a trees.

"Covenants were violated by noise, and the beauty of the area is lessened."

Damuel returned from the phone call to report that the "contractor is nervous about leaving his equipment. They may just leave and not return. They feel they have been used. They'll call tomorrow evening whether or not they'll finish the job."

Greedor explained a temporary restraining order and outlined his letter to J & J Development Company.

"1) No more trees cut then necessary for waterline.

"2) Slash must be cut into 12" lengths.

"3) Water line must be re-seeded.

"4) Jarvis & Company may use roads to do this."

"What are your charges for all this?" Curtis asked.

Greedor gave them a 50% reduction in hourly fees.

"One Hundred and twenty dollars to file in Federal Court. Then there'll be employment of legal witnesses, replacement costs, and appraisals of these costs."

Siefried wondered what the homeowners will recover. "Can we get into any trouble for this action?"

Ann Joslind said, "We should teach John and Judith a lesson that they can't get away with this."

"But we need to work towards a resolution and fair compensation for the homeowners," Siefried responded. "There's been a change in the properties. Geological hazards are possible."

A figure for expense for attorney's fees from homeowners was mentioned and Greedor to represent them approved.

In turn Greedor asked, "all homeowners for their cooperation in getting needed information to build our case."

Damuel summarized. "We have been damaged and experts are needed to assess the damages.'

Siefried was still questioning. "Can a lien be filed on the property prior to any damages that may be awarded?"

Damuel expressed "fear of obstructing a contract."

Watson expressed fear of reclamation and water. "I think we need a forestry expert."

"I will make sure J & J Development is given our conditions for logging and waterline, slash removal, and re-seeding taken care of," Greedor promised.

Damuel made a statement that J & J Development are in arrears on assessments and have no voting rights. Damuel dismissed the meeting.

CHAPTER 12
MARKHAM BUYS LOT 21

Robert Markhan stood alone on Lot 21 on Quiet Mountain surveying all the views in many directions. He had just finished a documentary film on the conservation and uses of water in the arid southwest. He didn't want an investment such as a ranch. Just a good-sized lot such as this, Number 21. Very private. Where he can come and go at will. On a free weekend. Maybe entertain close friends or business alliances. Something with a guest house away from the main house, and this lot could provide it.

There was a clearing on the lot as Judith had described. Sort of a meadow. It was just below boulders settled in the at the bottom of a slight rise or gentle cliff. The boulders served as a buffer from the mountain above.

In front of the clearing the juniper, pine and oak forest began again. Walking further northward the lot broke open on a rim. And what a view it was! Markham could look up the valley to the right and across at Rufe's Mountain with it's long slab of sandstone pointing upward toward the sky. He could look westward following the steep deep canyon cut by Beaver Creek. This view was almost too much for him. The upheaval was worrisome. "Maybe I'll get used to it," he thought. In the meantime he liked the sure upward slope of the sandstone to his right. It knows what it wants to do, he surmised.

He sat down on a boulder to soak in the beauty and awesomeness of what he'd found. A small lizard raced up the end of the boulder, stopped suddenly. Markham gently reached his hand toward the lizard. It scurried off. A wild rose was in bloom. He shot a closeup of the rose and another of the branch and rose. He looked over the rim again. There was the snag Judith had brought to his attention. He got up from the boulder to see the blue sky through its empty limb sockets. He aimed his camera wondering if he would match the venerable New Mexican painter's blue sky through skull sockets when to his surprise and delight a bald eagle came gliding slowly in and touched its feet to the top of the old pine and closed its wings and took possession of the snag. Markham walked around the base of the tall skeleton of the old pine and took the eagle from many angles. It made his day and settled the question. Yes, this was the place. Tomorrow he will draw up the contract with J & J and be on his way. He took more pictures for his architect and walked down to his car parked on the Jeep Trail.

Markham entered the lobby of the Grand Hotel. To the right was a small room that housed a collection of Victorian dolls and a Turn of the Century brocaded, gold fringed chair for him to rest in. An oriental rug covered the pine flooring. To the left of the entry was a small library with brocaded arm chairs and another oriental rug. This room focused on a heating stove with intricate laced steel housing complete with a steel footrest circling the stove to rest and warm one's feet when the snows are deep outside.

Markham passed them by and buzzed the elevator. He relaxed in his room, stretched out on an antique Victorian bed. He dozed and almost dreamed of what he'd found up on Lot 21 on Quiet Mountain. After a shower and change of clothes, he went out to eat. He stopped at the front desk to pick up messages.

There was a real estate guide, quite a sizable tabloid, with a cover in color, as well as a complete color section. The main feature was Quiet Mountain which John Sandstrom had put together. It included three color photos which John had taken. Judith had written the copy and worked with their realtor. It was well done and appealing.

Markham gave the feature a quick read and fell deeper in love which was what he wanted and anticipated. He now took his eyes off his lovely brochure of where his new home will be and looked at Joe Hendricks, the hotel owner, who was manning the desk. Markham sensed Hendricks had been watching him. There was amusement in Hendrick's face.

"I'd like to take this. I'm here to buy land. In fact, I think I've found what I want. I'm excited about it! Never in my wildest dreams did I expect to find such beauty!"

"Sure. Take it. That's what they're for. To be given and read. But you don't want to look at that subdivision! It's got all kind of problems."

"Not according to this feature."

"Yeah? Well just stay away from it, is my advice."

"Thanks. And thanks for the guide here."

Markham began making rounds to the local pubs to learn what he could about Quiet Mountain. He found newcomers knew nothing. Others knew there were problems. None could be specific. Markham didn't sleep well that night. Spent the restless night reasoning.

In the early morning hours he was able to set the problem aside, deciding to present his findings to J & J Development Company. Judith answered. John was in class.

"I'm coming over! I need to talk to you."

Upon arrival Markham burst out, "What the hell is going on?

I've been in town two days and if I mention buying a site in your development the heat is turned up right away as if it were a personal concern of everyone!

"I was showing your brochure to Joe Hendricks at the hotel and it was dead silence. After a while he says, 'There's a water problem up there.' I asked him what the problem is and he says, 'Don't know. But they've got a problem.'"

"How come you're adding a storage tank? Are you afraid of running out of water?"

"No. We feel pumping the tanks full and letting the water come down by gravity pull will be less wear and tear on the pump. Instead of turning it on and off so much. Also it's in position to service the next stage of development and the beginning of fire protection."

"What about the road? Is it travelable in winter?"

"These homes are occupied year round."

Markham began to feel amused. He did some surmising.

"What about money? Do you have enough to finish this project?"

"One more lot sale and everything is paid for. It's front loaded. No municipal district. Taxes and assessments are low."

Markham laughed lightly. "That's what I like to hear!"

"The last thing, besides the sillies of the altitude being too high to have flowers, when flowers grow at 9,500 feet or higher thirty miles north of here, is that the mountain is all land slide. Have you had any trouble with earth movement?"

Judith reached into her file cabinet and brought up a blue print of a large geographical quadrant map which included Quiet Mountain. It was fully mapped indicating rock fall, unstable slopes, potential unstable slopes, land slides, debris fans, mud flows, radioactivity, slop failure complex, seismic effect-faults, ground subsidence and snow avalanches.

Markham examined the mapping. It was put out by the State.

Now Markham really laughed with relief. He had almost been suckered in!

"If you're afraid of the mountains, go to the Mesas where there is shrinking and expanding clays," Judith told him.

Markham chuckled again.

In spite of the fact that Joe Hendricks advised Markham to stay away from Quiet Mountain, he wanted tall pines, that tremendous view, the primordial forest, everything Quiet Mountain had to offer. And closeness to town.

"I'm going to buy," he said. "I'd like to do it before I return. When can we sign? Tell me, do the locals pick on all the land for sale around here as they do your land?"

"Yes and no. We probably get it the heaviest. You see John teaches at the college and there is jealousy. At least my friends tell me that. I'm not able to comprehend educated people lying so much. I can't accept

it.   I don't want to live in that kind of
world.   It is what we bought the land for and
spent so much fun laying it out so that the
end result would be a lovely development with
genteel, neighborly, friendly people living in
it.   The contagion is spreading to the
purchasers in Quiet Mountain. They're behaving
as the outsiders."

Judith's voice had altered.   It could not
mask a deep disappointment and, as she said, a
perplexity she could not bear to face.

"Forget about that class of people!   I've
always had trouble with them!   And jealous
they are!   Way back in my youth in a
university in the East I had trouble with
them.   I was good with the camera even back
then.   It was a natural.   I was doing a good
documentary.   Had many letters of
recommendations on it.   We needed funding to

further promote it. You know it was turned down by the powers that be because they said 'it was over people's heads!' So I did a third grade level, mediocre thing, not appealing to either children nor adults, and they released the money. I walked out. That ended college for me... It's worse now than it was back then," he added.

"Yes," Judith answered, as images of Professors Bogg and Cog cluttered her mind. "That's why I dropped out of teaching and did something like this. But still it doesn't satisfy them," she said forlornly.

"They really hate, don't they?" Markham said.

"Yes," she answered as she thought of Tim, her nephew's current problems with the same Professors Cog and Bogg.

Leota Korns

"I received an *F* for exciting students over directing but not sticking to a lesson plan. Let's get the sale of Lot 21 over with and I'll be on my way."

CHAPTER 13

BURBANK'S SLEDGEHAMMER

Burbank's public address drew a hefty crowd in the Anglo-Indian College Ballroom. He had some very new and very interesting ideas on big Western projects. He had very straight white teeth!

Luna City had grown again since his last visit and the crowd was beginning to look more urban with Calvin Klein jeans, Anglos in moccasins with the wearer assuring the admirer he could order them from L. L. Bean, while another testified to the solidarity of her Range Rover.

Burbank told the crowd that existing projects all over the West were going to be reconfigured to give water back to the environment. "Change," he said, "must come quickly to melt the chains that bind us. The

171

era of dam building is over. There is enough
water if it is priced at its value. The
Bureau of Reclamation no longer will look to
water and power developers to direct and
support it. Efforts to enhance government
revenues will make farmers and other users
give up water."

There was a puzzled frown on Markham's face.
How? he wondered. Government doesn't own the
water! The states own the water!

Burbank almost answered Markham's puzzlement
personally as he continued his address.

"The traditional defenders of *the old water
world* are no longer in Congress. The Bureau
of Dams will become a resource manager rather
than a dam builder."

Burbank paused as if to remember he was in
the West. He added an explanation. "It's not
that the administration is against farmers and

ranchers, but it wants to go on the record as protecting the environment.

"Are there any farmers here?" he called. No hands were raised. He resumed his posture. "The number of dams in the American West is enormous. Should we take some down? The answer is yes. I would love to be the first Home Secretary in history to tear down a really large Western dam!"

There was a movement of people in their seats.

From this wish he went on to his intention of correcting one-hundred years of mistakes in land-use practices, including public lands grazing, mining, logging, and urban development.

Knowing now who his audience was, he promised, "If we can't get Congress to act we can enact the plan through regulations!

173

"I am a participant in this movement myself. I have swung ceremonial sledge hammers five times in the last 18 months. What is it about the sound of a sledgehammer that so seizes the imagination? An era is winding down! We overdid it building dams! We overdosed!"

Burbank's face was aflame with zealotry when Markham snapped his picture.

"We transformed rivers into water mains, irrigation canals and slackwater sumps, robbed our estuaries and deltas of needed nutrients, stole sediment from our ocean beaches, debased a part of our American heritage. At the same time, flood control—one of the main reasons for building many big dams—has become something of a joke. Flood damage in America has increased, not decreased, despite billions invested in dams."

Markham took a picture from a different angle. It disturbed Burbank somewhat but he was so carried away with his new mission of reversing one hundred years of improvement to civilization that he could hardly be detained even when he paused for questions and the farmers and ranchers began to question his positions.

"I lived in Kansas City in 1950 when the Kaw or the Kansas River flooded where it joined the Missouri River in what they call the West Bottoms where much manufacturing was located, including the stockyards and meat packing plants. There was no dam on the Kaw. It was only in the talking stage as a needed dam when the Kaw overflowed and created the devastating flood. I was working for a newspaper in a nearby town and examined the damage. Three story houses were turned over and moved from their basements. Livestock was caught in pens. The damage was enormous. The results were that a number of the packing companies moved out of Kansas City in disgust of no flood protection. Later the Kaw was damned for flood control. I have not heard of a flood in the heart of Kansas City since. What is so bad about a dam where it is needed or even if one is built like the many that are in Missouri for recreation—fishing, boating, water skiing, camping, swimming? That type of recreation is also a big industry. What do you see wrong with that?" John Sandstrom asked.

Burbank waited for the next question.

"Yes, lakes are far more recreational than unused rivers and the rivers can be used to the point of the dam!" said Matt Stahlek.

"And you say you're going to dismantle the Glen Canyon Dam? Why? Again you have all that recreation and the river is used for rafting before the dam. And you condemn the electricity furnished to all the smaller municipalities and farms in a large area of the dam? There is something wrong!" exclaimed Dennis Cameron.

"How about irrigation? There are more dams needed in the west for irrigation. Needed to store the water where the waters begin to use the snows as they slowly melt for irrigation. What's wrong with that?" demanded Arthur Stahlek.

"I've never heard of a delta being starved. The Mississippi delta used to be somewhere in Illinois. Now it's building on down into the Gulf of Mexico, way south of New Orleans.

Where do you get your information?" asked Elmer Jarvis.

"How about dismantling the Salt River Project feeding water to Phoenix? Why isn't that on your list?" asked Senator McGrevor.

Burbank stood his ground. He wouldn't attempt to answer any question. And on that, the evening was over and Burbank looked frantically for Carrie Moore, the publisher of the Luna City Times, hoping he could influence her. In the milling crowd, he searched over the heads of people for the sight of her as the talk began.

"They're going to have to give in to the *Greater Good*," Professor Brown declared as if he hadn't heard the questions either.

"People are still adjusting to dams anyway. Dams won't be hard for people to give up. I think he's right," said Professor Butler.

"And the Indians? How are they going to use the water? They'll just sell it. We might as well buy it and get the dam question settled."

"Yeah, I think you have a point."

"You know they never figure the cost of dismantling a dam when they build one. That's a cost that should be figured in on any dam under construction."

"Of course, the dismantling is part of the package!"

The salient point that caught and stayed with Egbert, Stan, Roland and Connie was the Home Secretary's wish to go down in history as the first person to tear down a really large Western dam. Much bigger than digging out a big, beautiful blue spruce! They talked a lot about it in the days that followed. The question was how to do it and do it *quickly*, how to *melt the chains that bind us* and insure irreversible success. They would study dams and how they're constructed. Coming from the Home Secretary there was nothing to fear.

It will take more than a leader with straight white teeth to save the West, Markham thought.

CHAPTER 14

MS. CARVER'S STUDENTS' PARENTS

Ms. Carver had three new poster pictures on her classroom wall. One given her by Ida Stahlek of their herd of cows and two that Robert Markham had shot. One, of the white headed eagle perched on the tall old Ponderosa snag on his Lot 21 and another of Arthur Stahlek and sheepherders bringing Arthur's band of sheep up from New Mexico to wait for shearing and lambing and shearing before traveling on north into the high mountains for summer grazing and growing new wool.

The sheep were a thousand strong, pristine white, fully rounded and pregnant. Markham's photo caught the sheep coming down from a gentle sloped brown dirt road cut through bluish sagebrush with dark green juniper, pinon and pine taking over in the background.

Arthur led the river of sheep, two sheep herders picking up the middle and rear of the long contingent. It was a striking, beautiful picture. The children loved it. Some had never viewed a band of sheep before and so beautifully displayed, their white wool against nature's green and brown background and the blue sky above.

There were oohs and aahs and spoken desires to take a field trip and get to play with these wooly creatures and maybe own a pet sheep.

"I didn't know sheep were so white and pretty," Eunice Easterly said. "I would love to touch one of them."

Ms. Carver brought the students' attention to the eagle. Johnny Sandstom said, "I know where that picture was taken!"

Ms. Carver said, "Yes, up on Quiet Mountain!"

"And now he can't build his house!" Johnny said with a tone of proprietorship and awe and no settled opinion.

"Why?" Losso Damuel asked.

"Because it will upset the eagle!" Johnny said in the same tone of wonderment.

"We had an eagle mounted on our living room wall but it's back in Chicago," Bobby Cameron shared.

Then slowly Ms. Carver approached the herd of cattle. "How many of you have been out driving along the highway and have seen cattle grazing in the field?"

Many hands went up.

"This is what Mrs. Stahlek's husband, Matt, does. He raises cattle. Do all of you like hamburgers?"

"Yeah! Yum Yum!"

"And beefsteak? And roast beef, mashed potatoes and gravy?"

"Yeah!"

"Well these meals come from cattle like these. And of course the milk we drink comes from cows too. I used to milk cows before and after school as part of my chores. But now it's done mostly by milking machines unless you have just a small acreage and milk one or two cows for your own family.

"I brought you a picture booklet of five pages of a cow which the Cattle Women's Association sent me. These are pictures of all the things a cow contributes to our lives. You may get up from you seats and collect in groups of five. I have enough of these booklets so that each group may have one.

Count off five and each group of five find a place to gather and look at these pictures."

The students made five groups and found space at the front of the room, the rear, and the middle aisle.

"Let's look at the first picture. What all do you see inset in this cow?"

"I see a car taking up its entire innards."

"On top of the cow is a two-story house."

"There's a telephone on the hood."

"And the cow is wearing sunglasses."

"In its belly is a large T-bone steak."

"A leather briefcase is coming from its upper rear leg."

"Bars of soap from the front leg."

"Crayons from the other lower rear leg."

"There's an airplane on top!"

"Are you surprised that so much comes from a cow?"

"But I don't know how it does!"

"At the bottom of this page it tells us that beef by-products enable us to use 99% of every beef animal. How much is that?"

"Quite a bit!"

"When you get into percentages you'll remember and know that's about all or 100%. We have four more pictures:

When Its A Meal

When It's A Household

When It's A Pharmacy

When It Gets Us There

Which do you want to look at next?"

"When it gets us there!" the boys called.

"Okay. What do you see?"

"A jetliner

"Tires

"And ball bearings in axle grease."

"Some I'd better read. Hydraulic brake fluid. Airplane lubricants and runway foam. Steel ball bearings containing bone charcoal. Car polishes and waxes. Textiles for car upholstery. Tires have stearic acid which makes rubber hold its shape. Glue from colloidal proteins has been used in automobile bodies. Even the asphalt on our roadways has a binding agent from fat."

Suddenly a loud clear voice from the back of the room called out, "That's all bullshit from the cattle industry who won't give up their cows so we can be COW FREE IN '93!"

Mrs. Easterly walked further into the classroom.

Ms. Carver glanced at her watch. It was almost dismissal time. "Students you may put the booklets on this desk and we'll finish studying them tomorrow. Put your books away and get ready to go home." Then she gave Mrs. Easterly attention.

"You really want to give up all that's on this brochure?"

"I took one look at it and it's not for me!"

"What do you mean it's not for you? You're a daily user of these products! Even if you walked here! I see you have leather shoes on your feet!"

"Who in the hell cares, Ms. Carver? Let them live with their cows! But just don't ask me to subsidize them! They've got more land now than they can swallow."

Mrs. Easterly departed with Eunice and Ms. Carver was called to the telephone in the office. She found another complainant and while on the phone, the door to the office blasted open and Darth Damuel stood there and said, "Get the hell off that phone and come in here and wait on me. Get your ass in here and give me Losso's lesson assignment for when we'll be gone next week."

Ms. Carver got free of the complainer on the phone and silently gave Damuel the schedule of homework. Out in the school yard, Ms. Carver doubled as a traffic director. Damuel bumped Ms. Carver with his BMW before he calmed himself and drove away with Losso.

The principal with a policeman had taken Damuel's license number. "We're going to suspend Damuel from the school ground for a week when they get back. We're starting to use the Orange County guidelines and penalties as of yesterday as passed by the Board of Education. There is no code for foul-mouthed students but we are suspending the parents. Longer on non-parents."

"Thank God for some relief," sighed Ms. Carver.

When Darth Damuel returned and faced the prospect of being suspended from the school grounds with his next outbreak, he and Mrs. Easterly and other friends in the Newcomers Club called for a public hearing on the new rules. It turned out to be a public forum wherein these new parents confronted the old or native community with their wants and demands which were more than likely in conflict with the established community as well as with themselves inwardly. It brought out the whole social structure:

Cattlemen/women's Associations, the loggers, sheep ranchers, developers to build homes for the newcomers, school teachers and administrators, professors from the college, bright students who were having difficulty in school and college, city and county governments, Indian Tribe representatives, and newcomers.

The newcomers complained of traffic in the school's parking lot wherein almost each student has hiser own car and the parking lot handling all the cars was ten times the size of the school buildings. They felt they were getting back to the road rage as bad as it was in California. "Where do we go next? they wondered. "We've bought land in Luna City to come to a place where we could walk in nature where no one else has ever walked before and what do we see? Sheep and cows!"

The ranchers burst out laughing. It made a pause in the proceedings.

The newcomers didn't understand the humor. "You don't believe me?" Mrs. Easterly exclaimed. "I took pictures of them. I'll show them to you! Here! Come and look at them!" She placed her pictures on the commissioners' table.

Darth rose and said, "All right! You've told us what you want suspended, we'll tell you what we want suspended. We want to get rid of cattle, sheep, no more development, no more dams, drain the big dam, give up rights to transplants in medicine from our neighbors, the animals, tell us where we can have the experience of camping where no one else has ever camped, give up some of your land, you own too much land, give up selling your land for greed, developing your land for greed, you can do anything you want because you own the land. Give up these exorbitant rights! There is no such thing as private property anyway!"

"I resent this! We can't do anything we please with our land! If you want us to give up something so vital to our life, what will you give up?" Arthur Stahlek asked.

"I resent all the homework my son has to do! Why all the memorizing? Why do your teachers think Shakespeare is more worthy than a baseball card? I help my son collect them!

"Why is science so emphasized? Isn't it just one among many cultures, and therefore has no more claim on truth than any other culture!" Summers, the baseball card collector, asked.

"It is impossible to find enduring universal truths in any area of investigation, and *reality* is chimerical or at best inaccessible to human cognition. Objectivity and truth are merely myths of our dying culture," announced Professor Albert Brown, of the science department.

One of the young college students who might have been one of the very bright ones in another cultural time spoke. "Our culture is doomed unless we destroy all technology, and the science that has produced it, and regress to a state occupied by the world's most backward countries. We must return to a tribal life wherein all was peaceful and everyone got along with each other."

Robert Markham endured the youth but addressed Professor Brown. "If you succeed in acquiring control of the curriculum, and then institute a kind of forced-conditioning of students with the literatures and ideological apologia for backward people, the consequence for the universities will be quite other then you foresee," he paused to observe the response of Brown who remained stoic. Markham continued, "The colleges of science will secede from their traditional association with the liberal arts colleges. That would be a tragic development not only for academia, but for all of society."

This was already ahead of the average meeting attendant. The most that could be delivered was from an embittered, frustrated and vitriolic boomer who retorted to Markham, "Come on, fella, help me out here. I will admit to being somewhat confused. I sense that it's not the yuppies or baby-boomers or environmentalists who fear their own mortality, it's you; and as eager as you seem to be to see the obituary written for the boomer generation and that danged environmental movement, I suspect it's really your own looming obituary that bothers you. After all, you're a lot closer to it than the younger generation, and it's your generation that has contributed the most to the sorry shape the world is in."

"Hikers should be potty trained! We didn't have giardia lamblia until these mountains got infested with hitch hikers burying their", Matt paused, "mess beneath six inches of top soil so that with the first rain it washed right down to the nearest stream to infect our wild life and now our domestic. Pack it out like you do when river rafting!" Matt said.

"How gross!"

"I have to explain to my child why Ida Stahlek protects her chickens but not her coyote and I can't explain it!"

"I don't own the coyote," answered Ida Stahlek. "The coyote does not need my protection!"

The native American, Rabbit Run, with the eagle feather still in his hat band, spoke to the racist issue of presupposing Indians did not inhabit the land in presettlement times. "For me, I see the misanthropic implications of the Wildlands Project which Frank Frankel co-founded and which would remove or severely limit the activities of people from nearly half the land in America. Then who would own the land? The federal government like in an Aristocracy or a Karl Marx Socialism, or a dictatorship, or the impossible tribal system of the young man's desire? Does Frank Frankel think the environmentalists alone could own, hold, manage and care for the land?"

But none of the parents who had come lately to outcome based education dared rebuke Rabbit Run. Instead they voiced what they had been taught. "We should all get along. No one and no thing is of more worth than to the other thing."

197

There was a quiet moment as people tried to figure out this equation.

"Did you read the letter in the Earth News of the Luna Times Daily that the cow has four stomachs? The letter writer called it a Super Stomach. It digests and converts all types of vegetation indigestible by humans, into energy and important *building blocks* of the body. Humans cannot utilize vegetation efficiently, and therefore these potentially valuable resources would be wasted if we didn't get them from another source."

"I've heard enough!" Mrs. Easterly said, gathering up her pictures from the commissioners' long table.

The chief commissioner quietly told the packed meeting room, "Other people have rights too." Then quietly but clearly he asked Ms.

Carver, "What was your idea to be gained from this meeting?"

"After they called the meeting I hoped it would do some of the things I was trying to do in the classroom—teach the newcomers about the country they've chosen for their new home and also have them teach the students they've chosen to be their new neighbors what the country was like that they left. But we've not gotten to hearing about the areas the newcomers have come from." The frustrated boomer leaving, called back to the crowd, "We're outnumbered! But we won't always be outnumbered!"

CHAPTER 15

THE EAGLE TURNS MARKHAM INTO A CRIMINAL

William Foreman, Markham's architect, walked Lot 21 and fell in love with the lot as Markham had. He made suggestons to Markham which Markham thought made good sense and Markham flew back from California to confer with Foreman. They walked the lot together, dreamed and created Markham's mountain home. They rested a while on the boulder and enjoyed the peace. They watched the eagle and his mate fly back to their new nest high on the snag, and Markham took more pictures.

The house would be a beautiful structure. Foreman had an enviable reputation in California, Hawaii, Arizona and now he was considering a setting in Colorado. Markham returned to Southern California and Foreman proceeded with all the requirements—soils tests, topography, elevations, drainage, solar. Finally he was ready to take the package to the Building Department.

Foreman was in good spirits and happy to be selected to build a home on beautiful Quiet Mountain. The Building Department Supervisor thought the plans looked very good. He was impressed with Foreman and said he was glad Foreman was going to make his home in Luna City also. "These mountains need good design," he said. He showed the plans to the building inspector who'd just arrived in the office from a field inspection. He went over the package with the field inspector who also shared his satisfaction.

"On what lot in Quiet Mountain will this be built?" the inspector asked.

"Twenty-one," Foreman told him.

"Hmmmm. Wasn't there something that just came in recently on that lot?" "I don't know," answered the supervisor. "Maybe you'd better look it up."

"Here it is! Wildlife notified us last week. A pair of bald eagles have been spotted nesting up there!"

"They're nesting in a snag on the rim. They're beautiful to watch. They make everything worth the trouble," Foreman said.

"Yes," the supervisor said hesitantly. "But Wildlife rules will severely limit you in what you can do up there. I doubt if you can build the type of house your plans call for. Get that eagle management plan and let Mr. Foreman look at it."

The inspector went to an adjoining room and returned with a file folder a half inch thick.

"The bald eagle is listed on the Endangered Species list. You have to follow the Wildlife Management Plan. It's pretty well spelled out in this booklet." He handed it to Foreman.

Foreman scanned the contents table, then turned to each chapter to peruse the headings.

"You'll have to sign up on this plan and abide by it," the supervisor said. "You will need to have a copy. They're eight dollars apiece. There will be a filing fee when you're ready to begin."

"This damned thing is 32 pages long!" Foreman told Markham via phone. "There's hardly any space on the two acres that we can build. We've got to camouflage everything we do, to hide it from the eagles perched up there 80 feet above us.

"We've got to set a row of evergreens in front of the rim. They've got to be transplants and tall enough that the eagles can't see us or we them.

"It will rule out your view entirely.

"There's a stiff penalty if we don't accomplish this to the fullest. Very large fine and even jail time.

"I read it carefully last night."

"I didn't expect anything like this," Markham spoke slowly. "Let me call you back."

Markham slowly kept absorbing the square hit to the middle. Burbank was first to come to mind. "If we can't get Congress to act, we can enact the plan through regulations!"

"The sonofabitch," he said aloud.

Markham called Judith and John to tell them he might not be able to build his mountain home on Lot 21. He wondered if they knew about eagles.

No, they didn't. But they knew that Damuel has told the homeowners he is going to stop all lot sales on Quiet Mountain. They hadn't heard how he's going to do this but maybe the bald eagle is how. "He's got a large feather in his Western hat that he claims is a bald eagle's. He says he got it nearby."

"Well Markham wasn't told he couldn't build. It's only Damuel's desire to stop all sales," Judith said to John.

"Let him try!"

Markham took the evening to consider what he'll do. He saw a good documentary there in the mountains. These are the kinds of things he'd been reading about and hearing rumors of. He hadn't expected to be caught in the middle of them. He didn't at all like Burbank's talk. Only a damned fool would want to dismantle a Western dam and wreak so much havoc in the water scarce West. The man must not have any sense at all! But so many supporters! Bizarre!

Then he read a *Wall Street Journal* news piece on a Congressional filibuster on the Federal Government trying to take water from the Western Private Sector.

By morning Markham was gradually realizing this was a big problem. He was beginning to consider shelving the project he was working on and turn his attention to the problems in Colorado and the West.

CHAPTER 16

JOHN SANDSTROM'S DEATH

Judith told John that Francine has received a letter from Greedor, the Homeowners' attorney. The homeowners want the two largest lots deeded to them to take care of the damages from the logging. They also want no more lots sold in Quiet Mountain.

"They want to take all. They want to shut us down."

"Let them try!" John said.

"Francine said asking for two lots weakens their case."

"I'm going up to check the waterline. Maybe I'll trim some of the logs and get firewood for the winter. I'll take the truck and bring a load down."

It was quiet now where the homeowners had been marching. John was alone on the

207

mountain. He loved the land and particularly the solitude. If it weren't for trimming the logs he'd be walking the mountain way up high and exploring. That was the part he especially loved. To walk it, to plan it, to protect it, to eventually plant things on it. He still thought a good plan, good covenants, would bring peace and tranquility. He wondered when they get ahead enough to live up on the mountain if reality will be as good as the dream. He and Judith drove up often in all seasons and visualized life up on the mountain and wondered when it will ever happen for them. Three years ago, after selling all three lots that they liked, they chose a lot way out of the way of progress. They cut a service road into it, cleared a house and picnic area. They now entertain on it. It is a beautiful lot. It blooms in the virgin forest like a James Fenimore Cooper sunlit glade. A wilderness cathedral opening to the heavens. John and Judith were always conscious of a higher power guiding them. They had become one with the universe. John hoped this feeling would carry over to the homeowners too.

The sun was setting as John approached the water line. He hoped the homeowners were enjoying their evening dinner. He placed the power saw low to cut a large gambel oak in the water line extension. There was the abrupt sharp shrill sound of metal. The saw flew out of his hands, whirled back, and sawed into his face across his right eye. He was on the ground bleeding profusely. The saw was some distance away and the motor had chewed in the earth and stopped.

Damuel heard the sound of the saw and was on his way to inspect where the sound came from. John was unconscious and in his last moments when Damuel arrived. Damuel took John's pulse. It was over. He saw the spike and worked it loose from the tree and pocketed it. He couldn't hide the accident. He could suggest that John must have tripped, stumbled, or had an attack, or was just clumsy. And didn't wear a helmet.

Damuel walked down to his home to call for help. An accident! He ascertained it will be easier to stop sales. One half is out of the way. It will be easy to muscle in on Judith. The accident happened next to Lot 21, one of the lots to be serviced by the water line. Markham went up early next day to look at the scene. He examined the tree, found the hole left by the spike but he could not find the spike. He hoped it might yield a fingerprint but there was no spike to be found.

Egbert and Stan felt exhilaration at having achieved a real CD again. It was so successful that Egbert wanted to hit the papers with it but Stan and Roland prevailed and calmed him down. Egbert felt thwarted again. No punishment, and no recognition dimmed his whole achievement. It agitated him. Old actions like the egg throwing lingered and dimmed whatever attention he strove for. But they were successful in the spiking and it was exhilarating. Yet they were not recognized for the achievement as a Mother Green! Frank Frankel would have been. No one will be hearing about them. Egbert chafed in vexation of not belonging.

It was easy for Damuel to press the law to go along with the problem that John was not wearing a helmet. This was murder but the law and the press were willing to accept it as an accident. The hole in the oak and the saw's teeth failed to activate the police. And the citizenry was so zonked on the environment that there was no protest. In fact, in the muddled minds of the people it was best not to play it in the media because publicity was what Damuel and the environmentalists wanted.

The homeowners made no response to Judith at the time of John's death. Damuel orchestrated this. The law acceded without investigating that it was an accident and John should have been wearing a helmet. No one investigated the condition of the saw but Markham did and had pictures of the saw's missing teeth.

Ordinary people were convinced John and Judith were greedy to develop Selene Mountain and had it coming to them.

John's fellow professors went along with this also. Just his immediate department came to his funeral.

However, there were others who responded differently. An adjacent land owner who Judith really didn't know, called to say, "I'm so glad you folks didn't let them stop you when they asked the county commissioners to stop you from developing Quiet Mountain. It did my heart good."

Another neighbor called to say, "I thought your plan sounded so good at the meeting in the courthouse that I could not understand what the objection was all about."

The government had not ruled that Markham could not walk, sit, stand or sleep on his land so Markham started studying eagles. He became fascinated by them. He ordered books on eagles from UCLA and the University of California libraries. A new retroactive surprise law had come from Washington. Its salient points were printed in the paper. It was called the *Bionomic Domicile Guard Act*. Markham felt he had been made a near-criminal by this Act. The Act was very overreaching. He cannot harass, harm, pursue, hunt, shoot, wound, kill, trap, capture or collect a listed species. Nor their feathers. He cannot have an eagle feather in his possession. He cannot log, disk, or burn. There was now a $100,000 fine and a year in jail for cutting a tree. One of the stipulations was a *Significant Stress Area* around the eagle's nest, a radius of one point one half miles. This took in all of Quiet Mountain, a big part of Selene Mountain and the valley below.

Burbank had set up a *Bionomical Reconnaissance* to seek more creatures to save. He wanted entire ecosystems listed. The new law could apply anywhere to anyone across the United States.

Markham thought Burbank's ulterior motive was not to protect creatures but to extend the power of government. Quiet Mountain could now be spied on by the Federal Government. It spread. No one reacted. Defense of property was left to people like the Stahlek family and affected neighbors.

Damuel wondered if there might be another feather up on Lot 21. He undertook to win favors for himself and get by. The new law soon affected the Stahleks, Jarvises, Camerons. Even Ms. Carver and what she taught. Everyone who didn't exist in a cement environment was subject to being spied upon.

Markham was particularly watched by the government because he was in the cinema and these people do strange things. He was particularly watched if he might be growing marijuana, and carrying too much cash.

Many occupations—developing, ranching, farming, logging, cattle raising, sheep—had become looked upon as bad for the environment. People in these occupations were now victims of moral exclusion and deemed to live outside the pale of humanity to which moral values, rules, and considerations of fairness apply. The press was largely indifferent to the loggers, developers, and builders of homes for people. Activists called loggers *buffalo hunters, destroyers, tree murderers, and rapers of the land.* Moral exclusion of those who were accused of harming or abusing the environment was one of the most prominent expressions of the culture of environmental preservation. Ideas start quietly in the minds of ordinary people.

CHAPTER 17
JARVIS AND SON STEVE

It was true Hank Burbank didn't have to bother with the Congress. The regulatory layer of government did the job for him. He, alongwith the director of the Department of Bionomics, Christine White, created the new tool, the *Bionomic Domicile Guard Act,* which gave them the right to shut down land without bothering with the cost and time involved to find endangered species on the land.

This act made every place in the law where the expression *endangered species* appears to be followed by their *domicile.* Authorities could now regulate a property merely by declaring that it constitutes nebulous *domicile* for the creature of their choice. They no longer need to find an endangered creature there.

There was opinion that this device permitted authorities to stop a landowner from using his or her property until he or she sets aside another parcel for preservation to appease the regulators.

Robert Markham quickly knew it would always be one more parcel to satisfy the greed of the environmentalists and their regulators.

So did Darth Damuel. And that was why he began figuring a way to circumvent or politic his way around the law.

It would be very expensive for the Stahleks who need much land in the west to produce a living without irrigation water if they are forced to set aside a parcel or stop ranching because of the new law.

One news release was of Houghton, a rancher, on whom Burbank's Home Department in Washington made an on-the-grounds

219

demonstration to environmentalists of the benefits resulting from the funding levels the Home Department had supported.

Houghton's grazing permit was revoked and 150 head of his cattle confiscated at gunpoint. James Rancor, attorney, for the American Wildlife Association was quoted in the news advising activists that they could now win by "making it so expensive for ranchers that they go broke."

Meanwhile the Department of Timber Maintenance shared information on Houghton's eviction with attorney, Newman, of the National Insurance Company, who owned the Houghton's mortgage. Houghton missed a mortgage payment and National Insurance Company foreclosed. Markham noted that National Insurance Company contributes to American Wildlife Association.

Judith, reading the news, realized she was up against a government-industrial-environmental coalition. Markham visiting her told her to make the list longer, the government-industrial-environmental-educational-media-legal coalition. "It's leading us to a caste society," he said. "The poor can be attacked with impunity. Neither the Democrats, who've sold their souls to the environmentalists, nor the Republicans, who won't fault the rich, will help the individual."

Judith gave a quick, downward motion of her head. "It's a bad situation."

However, concurrently, a Federal Appeals Court made a ruling favoring logging. Jarvis learned of the Federal Appeals Court Ruling through his Loggers' Association. The law will allow *salvage* logging of wide areas of old-growth forests without environmental restrictions. The new law, known as the *salvage rider* allowed logging of 4.5 billion board-feet of timber on federal lands nationwide without environmental restrictions, other than those already applied by government officials. Much of it was timber that had been killed or damaged by forest fires and insects, but it also included green timber.

This was of great interest to Jarvis. It was what he had been waiting and praying for. He will now have at least two years of steady work for his crew.

Young Steve Jarvis returned home for the summer from Atlantic League campus full of ecology curricula. He never associated his father with an anti-environmentalist as they were portrayed to him in college. Upon arriving in town he called up his childhood friend, James Murray, and James was in full preparation to join a protest against the new Federal Appeals Court Ruling. Steve quickly decided not to miss the protest for anything in the world.

Elmer Jarvis had the logging contract for the area that was to be protested. It was close to home and easily worked and Jarvis was thankful. Jarvis' loggers had been idle and while getting that portion of the Jarvis business back together Jarvis himself would man a bulldozer cutting a skid path, and sometimes a loader and a skidder until more loggers returned.

Jarvis looked forward to the summer with Steve at home. He was sure Steve and Cameron would strike it off fine and there'd be plenty of work for Steve this summer.

Jarvis was not the foremost of the Dr. Spock child training parents but he accepted Spock's theories and he and his wife, Joyce, tried to apply them in raising their two children. And Steve, the first-born, probably got the most concentrate of the Spock-Jarvis raising. The vision, after World War II, was to make a better world and what better place to start than with one's own children. Eliminate the emotional blocks, the scars, the hang-ups. Open the windows and let the sun shine in!

Elmer and Joyce Jarvis were good parents. Nothing extreme like the Danish Easterly family with their screaming, abusive daughters, and Egbert who wanted to taste physical punishment.

The Jarvises tried always to be teaching and guiding and setting a good example. Like the time Steve hastily set a heavy iron skillet atop the refrigerator while helping his sister, Marcella, finish dishes so that she could play short stop in a baseball game about to begin.

The skillet was too close to the edge and when Joyce opened the refrigerator door the heavy skillet fell, knocking the lowest shelf off the refrigerator door. It was the tall bottom shelf that Joyce put the tall bottles on. She didn't want to give it up and was drawing designs to replace it. She had called the manufacturer and received part of the shelf but nothing to fasten it into the door.

Joyce was annoyed with what had been sent her. Elmer could see she was trying to re-invent the door. Joyce could see no other way but to rebuild it. Elmer looked at the door and found a solution at the same time. "Wait until the ballgame's over. I think I can fix it."

When dinnertime approached, he called Steve and Marcella in to repair the door. Steve was going on eight and Marcella seven.

"Steve, you bring the hack saw and my drill and Marcella you bring some screws and a screwdriver."

"Now what?" Joyce asked.

"I think we can fix the door with the shelf they sent you."

The children arrived back.

"Now Steve, hand me the broken off shelf over there and we'll saw a piece out of it. Can you measure how deep the new shelf is?"

Four inches was Steve's measurement.

"We need to take a four inch piece of the old shelf and use Marcella's screws to fasten it to the new shelf."

That was done. Joyce looked in amazement of how Elmer could figure out mechanical things.

"Now let's drill a hole into the refrigerator door facing and with screws fasten this end of the shelf to the door by way of our little strip. Then we'll do the other end. Marcella we'll need the drill and the screws and the screwdriver. Now it's done! It's stronger then it was originally and Mama can put the things back into the refrigerator. Steve and Marcella, you put the tools back as you found them."

Joyce was all smiles. Elmer had made it so simple!

And Steve, also, was eager to effect change upon society and the world. Steve was surprised how far James had gotten into ecological science remaining in the West while he'd been in the East. In fact, James was a greater disciple than Steve. James knew of Egbert's crowd but hadn't made contact with them first hand.

Both James and Steve were marching for the good of America. James believed his generation's protests' results would be good because their intentions were so good. James sold Steve on the idea of protesting. Steve wanted to experience it and James further enhanced it. James' fervor justified the excitement which lay ahead. "It's the right and responsibility of every citizen to question the unjust policies and actions of his or her government. Nothing is more uniquely, traditionally, and beautifully American than peaceful protest."

Steve moved easily into James feelings. He had turned in a paper in Earth Science which sounded identical to James' feelings. He had received an A on that paper.

"The notion that protests somehow cost the taxpayers money, as the Department of Timber Maintenance asserts, is ludicrous," James intoned. "A logical extension of this thinking is that elections should be banned because they are so expensive to hold.

Democracy is a messy business."

Steve didn't quite follow that but he let it pass.

The forest was lovely. Ancient pine snags were easily spotted. Many logs were down across old lumber trails. There was much dead timber that would be cut into to determine if it was salvageable for lumber. Much of the old was rotted in the center. But there were also mature trees to be felled. There was excitement and expectation from both the loggers and the protestors.

Egbert, Stan, Roland, Connie and Hubert were in the cordoned off area of the forest. Cordoned off by Forest police for the containment of the protestors. Protestors chained themselves to cattle guards, in trees, lay in the roadways and held hands across gates. The Forest police kept clearing the area for work and herding the protestors into the cordoned off area. The logging crews now readied for work. Jarvis climbed into the cab of a bulldozer. Cameron would collect the logs as they were felled and limbed. He would skid them down to the loading area. Another would load them onto the logging trucks.

James and Steve had locked hands and lay across the cattle guard, each chained to a guard post. The bulldozer slowly moved along the newly built road toward where the cutting would begin. The Forest police were busy sawing chains from trees, removing spikes as they spotted them, searching protestors for more locks, herding protestors away from the work area and back to the protest area cordoned off for them. Two were assigned to ordering two remaining tree protestors out and down from trees. Jarvis approached the bodies on the ground. He looked for police aid but all police were busy. Jarvis inched the bulldozer closer. It would be a game of nerves. James was wondering if he'd be brave enough to give up a leg as Frankel had done in the Northwest timber battles.

"Move!" Jarvis shouted.

There was no movement from Steve or James. Jarvis swung the bulldozer to the right to proceed over the barrow ditch and through the

231

trees.   Steve and James got to their knees.
Steve was nearest the barrow ditch.   He lay
down and stretched his legs as far out over
the barrow ditch as possible.   Jarvis started
to swing the cat to the other post.   Then he
recognized it was Steve over the barrow ditch.
He stared right into the eyes of his son whom
he hadn't seen since Christmas.   He choked.
He realized he'd been expecting an eighteen-
year-old and that time has been lost to him.
Steve was twenty-four now.   Jarvis choked
again.   A great feeling of unfairness engulfed
him.   This was not what he and Joyce planned
when they stood against the family and let
Steve have a choice in almost everything,
patiently explaining the probable end result
of each decision the son was making.   Steve
was far ahead of his peers in taking

responsibility for his actions. What's wrong with him now?

Jarvis was slowly becoming convinced the protestors were not thinking things through. He'd been able to believe the young people would change once they got out into the world and faced reality. But how far could he go in his leniency and yet not destroy his neighbors and himself nor deny the younger children in his family?

He was trying to sift all this in his mind and once and for all get control of his ambivalence when a shout, "Stop!" brought him to a jolt. The bulldozer was almost touching the chained body.

The chained Steve had no key to the chain's lock. The sheriff's deputies came with a chain saw and sawed through a link of the chain.

Cameron came. "I'll take over!" he called out to Jarvis above the noise of the caterpillar. Jarvis was still staring into the face of his son. The son stared at his father in disbelief. He could not comprehend that his father was one of *them*. His father linked with big lumber, big oil and gas, big coal production! His ideal of doing something uniquely, traditionally and beautifully American... He had never in any of his wildest dreams when hearing of the protests in college, or planning the protest with James and tasting the protests' satisfying exhilaration, thought his patient, responsible father to be on the other side. He never remembered his father to have that razor-sharp thinking so that he could be comfortable with *multinational conglomerate drilling for natural gas on our National Forests.* In fact,

Steve never questioned who owned the national forests beyond James' group of protestors. And James said he was protecting the forest against everyone who was against the forests. All Steve had ever envisioned the actions of *them* to result in was a vast industrial zone in this national forest and receiving government subsidy to make it so.

As is recommended in the U.S. Constitution, we peacefully assembled.

Jarvis was believing he must be more razor-sharp like his brother-in-law. *I am no enemy sure to run over them. No Russian military with orders to kill! He is the product of my genes and my raising. My spoiled offspring raised permissively.*

"You Baby Boomers have to be responsible for your own pampered, selfish behavior just like our generation and all the other generations had to be responsible for their faults." Cameron's voice came booming after he shut down the caterpillar. "You belong to the White Male Movements. You skipped the Indian Movement, the Hispanic Movement, the Black Movement, the Women's Movement, and the Labor Movement. They are of too long duration to satisfy your appetite for Civil Disobedience.

"You're a generation that hates or dislikes its parents, feels no obligation towards its parents, only wants more from its parents!" Cameron had run out of steam.

Then he thought of the recent protest demanding the man needing a liver transplant from a baboon, to die in place of the baboon. "You are evil!" he shouted. "You hate your own species!"

Cameron helped Jarvis out of the cab. Jarvis was overcome with guilt, remorse, confusion, disappointment. What went wrong with his best intentions? He wanted his children not to have the hangups which have plagued the human race from the beginning of time. He used the best of experts. Now an inner voice which he hadn't yet been able to recognize, to give expression to, something beginning to be felt... He and Joyce had cheated their children of knowledge, and their children had to manufacture their own difficulties and reject what he had so sacrificed to give them.

The sheriff had sawed through Steve's chain and Steve was standing up and stretching his legs which had gone partially asleep. Jarvis was on the cattleguard. Steve turned to walk away. Jarvis took Steve by the shoulder and turned him around.

"I raised you, son. I did a bad job of it. I apologize. I raised you by cheating you of life's experiences. Now, I don't know how you'll get them. Except as you're doing. Destroying civilization."

We cheated our children of the knowledge of life, he thought sadly. You and I, Joyce. We're a sad lot.

"It's done now, Steve. Neither of us can go back. But I'm sorry. I made a bad decision."

Tears streamed down Jarvis' face. Steve was overwhelmed. He couldn't touch his father. His comrades called, "Come on!"

Steve pulled away from his father.

"Go, son, if it's what you have to do. Go, and get it over with."

Then we can rebuild, he thought sadly.

He turned from his son to climb back into the bulldozer.

"Wait!"

Steve ran to his father and embraced him.

"I don't know you! I thought it was your kind who were destroying the planet. We were trying to save it!"

"Save it for yourself, son! Think what you're doing! For yourself! How will you win?"

Then Jarvis' eyes clouded over and he looked away from Steve.

"We are guilty," he said to himself. "We broke a universal law in trying to change human nature. *Nature is*. Like the Greeks learned. You can't outwit the Gods."

A Forest policeman on a horse bent forward and took a picture of Steve's astonished face.

CHAPTER 18
MARKHAM COMFORTS JUDITH

"Jim", Steve Jarvis said, "I can't go on with these protests. I can't turn against my father and mother. I have no quarrel with them. I do think the forest in it's condition is dangerous. An uncontrollable, very hot fire waiting to happen. I'd like to show the students back east at Atlantic League what this forest is really like—the dangers, the wasted wood product. But I fear they'll not listen, nor try to understand. I haven't told my father and mother yet but I don't plan to go back to Atlantic League. I don't need what so many of those classes teach. I'd like to be the friend we've always been before these protests."

"I'm not ready to quit," James Murray said. "But I can understand your feelings towards your parents. I'm committed to our country. To make it a better place with more opportunity for those who aren't so rich."

"We're not rich," Steve said quietly.

James proceeded with the protests. He didn't join Egbert's group but kept his membership in the Sonora Club, kept active in Mother Green! And kept reading and soaking up the religious tracts he was sent.

Steve settled into his bedroom at his parents' home and signed on for work with his father's logging contract. He would make one more of the former logging crew back at work.

Being home he heard of Ms. Carver's despair of trying to teach students of many of the new people moving into the area and of her resignation from the school district and of her plan to establish a private school. She had a number of students registered and was looking around for help. Steve contacted her and they had many mutual experiences to share. He was happy that she was going to do something new and hopefully healthy for the country. Next winter he would help her and be on her staff.

Judith took her camera and went up to Quiet Mountain. She paced how far the saw flew from where John was cutting. She took a picture of the partially cut oak and a picture of the ruptured grass where the saw dug into the earth. She had brought flowers and a simple wooden cross to mark the spot where John was felled. Cameron had made the cross for her and he fashioned it in Hispanic carving and paint. She thought of naming a trail after John and having some kind of monument built but wondered if the homeowners would destroy it.

She sketched a map and took measurements of where the accident happened.

Later she rested on a nearby boulder and remembered how she and John would find a suitable boulder to rest and often lie on the mountain, to take an afternoon nap, using their shoulder cases of tagging, compass, tape line, stakes, hand level and maps underneath their heads as a pillow. She wanted to commune with John. It was in this quiet time that Robert Markham approached. He had been up on Lot 21 with his bird books and camera. He had seen Judith but respected her vigil. He would now pay his respects. He had found another eagle feather and had it in his hat band. He was curious how the eagle and other birds of prey soar or sail on air currents larger that the oceans. Is it something in the wing?   What gives the eagle such immense power?

It was against the law for him to be in possession of the feather, or any bird or bird part, punishable by up to six months in jail and a $5,000 fine under the Birds of Prey Treaty Act.

The Indian tribes had learned this and the law was much publicized.   There were now over 1,000 species listed and the list covered almost everything except common starlings and pigeons.   Because of the law it was difficult for Indians to obtain bird feathers and parts for religious purposes.   In order for Indians to get parts from bald and golden eagles, they must prove that they were enrolled members of a federally recognized tribe, then add their names to a waiting list with the Fish and Wildlife Caretakers' National Eagle Repository in the Northwest. Then wait as much as two years.

Sometimes an Indian was not that familiar with the law and would give or receive feathers as an act of faith to gain wisdom and strength from the spirits of the birds.

Sometimes the government, itself, was very confused on the myriad of laws relating to birds. It was rumored that double-train war bonnets were bringing $20,000 on the black market.

The media reported that most Native Americans didn't like the delays but were more willing to live with the delays than they were with non-Indians getting these feathers and not them.

But Rabbit Run, caught with an owl and vulture feathers in his hat while performing a traditional song for students, and the local

Indian woman, White Cloud, who gave them to him, learned that both may have broken the federal law and their punishment was being reviewed.

Rabbit Run said there was an injustice in the system. "I have to have a permit by federal law even to have a feather. Yet I can go dig up a grave, and it's only a misdemeanor. That bothers me, that our birds require more respect than human beings."

Rabbit Run said he intended to keep handling eagle feathers in religious services to rebury Indian dead disturbed by looters even though he didn't have a permit.

Markham had gathered his sack of books, camera and binoculars. "I would like to interest you in what I'm doing with Lot 21. I feel I even might be stopped from studying eagles. Wouldn't it be awful if the great

United States imprisoned us away from all knowledge and we truly lived in darkness?"

He had caught Judith's attention so he quoted Matthew Arnold. "'And we are here as on a darkling plain Swept with confused alarms of struggle and flight, Where ignorant armies clash by night.'

"I've decided to study my renter, the eagle, or the captive, myself. Look at this picture of an eagle wing! A marvel of natural engineering! It is extremely light, structurally strong, easily repaired or replaced when damaged. It's not rigid like an aircraft's wing."

Judith wiped her eyes and looked at the picture.

"We tried to plan it good and orderly so that it would be a lovely place to live and create like you're doing and like we had planned to do. But there is so much emotional violence—." She could not speak more. Finally, she asked, "What is the cause of it? What is to be gained?"

"Right now, I feel nothing," said Markham. "That's why I'm using my time to study my captor."

He showed her pictures of the saw with the broken teeth and the hole in the gambel oak left by the spike.

"John was killed," she said quietly, firmly. Her moist eyes changed to a wrinkled brow. "Why?"

"It is the time we live in. The spirit of conflict. Disruption. Childishness. Who can play with me and my ball and who can't play with me and my ball. We have lost the spirit of this country... We have no spirit. Just free floating anger in all directions. No great needs and wants. The void is filled with the excitement of destruction. You and I are out of sync or we could be killing and maiming too and celebrating it."

"I can't take it. I don't want it. I don't want to live this way. I'm afraid to set the flowers down. To put a fragile marker up. They will be destroyed. It's my land. I have no right on it!"

Markham put his arm around Judith's shoulder. "I know," he said.

He took the wooden cross and the hammer and drove the cross into the ground by the partially cut gambel oak and then set the flowers in their container beside the cross.

"May God grant John rest!" he said. "Don't worry! Sooner or later order will be restored. That is all we can have faith in now. Go with me to dinner. It will do you good. We can remember John together. I, of course, did not truly know him but I'd be glad to hear about him if at any time you would like to tell me."

But Judith was not only in shock and sadness but confused, trying to do right in an immoral society. Her feelings were very tender. She could see no end to trouble. She realized how she's been robbed of the water system to serve John and her lot as well as Markham's and the others. She wanted to run from the mess but didn't know where to run. She felt betrayed and cheated. She couldn't think any longer.

So they went to eat at the River's Edge Cafe along the river's bank and Robert talked about his life and experiences and Judith listened.

"This is a far cry from my childhood in South Dakota in the Black Hills near Mr. Rushmore and the hills where Crazy Horse is being carved. That is a dream too. Korczak won't take any federal money. He wants the people to pay for it through donations. Have you ever been to Mr. Rushmore?"

"No."

"You must go. It might restore some faith. Those four presidents--Washington, Jefferson, Lincoln--it should have been the last Roosevelt, the paralyzed one, who led us through the Great Depression and World War II. You look up to them and you get used to the act of standing still in the presence of freedom and democracy. Raw granite beauty that both humbles and inspires. Mr. Rushmore is the birthplace of awe. My birth state of South Dakota is filled with historical change. My own ancestors lived in small sod houses. Patriotism and the Mt. Rushmore sculptures are a part of my growing up. And Korczak's Crazy

Horse is also one of heroic bravery in the face of abrupt change and defeat.

"There is this generation passing from us, leaving us with a great heritage. I want to do something to commemorate them. That generation who survived the Great Depression and fought to keep Europe and America free. They ask no thanks. They will not walk this earth much longer. This was going to be my next project before the eagles entered into my life. We had eagles in South Dakota too. The rich prairies of South Dakota, Wyoming and northern Colorado. Hundreds of miles of open space. Grasslands. That's what I'm used to. And the sculptures."

"I grew up in Western Oklahoma. And still the West was out there!" she stretched her full arm westward, "a place of vastness, a place you dreamed of to go and '*let the rest*

of the world go by, a place of perfect peace.'
My early childhood in Western Oklahoma! My
brother, Dan, and I rode horses all day long.
Did errands on horseback. We worked in the
fields, shocked wheat, milked cows, raised
chickens. I sold spring chickens, pullets, to
pay for piano lessons. I would carry a spring
chicken, feet tied together in a gunny sack.
Stop at the poultry, beef, and pork
processing, sell the chicken and walk on to my
piano teacher. We learned patience. Who do
you know who's learned patience?"

"The rancher."

"I never saw a thousand band of sheep as out
here making the spring journey to the
mountains nor the fall journey to New Mexico.
That's new to me. But I like it! I don't
hate the rancher."

"Neither do I. I see no freedom here. It's a far cry from my childhood in South Dakota. The promise is here in the millions of acres of uninhabited mountain ranges but it's more and more denied us. And the people are not being represented. In fact, they're not wanted. I'm not wanted! You're not wanted! And many others! I also liked the immense distances of the prairies of the Dakotas and Wyoming. Most is owned by people. Not like here where government owns most of it and certain groups want to rule all."

"After the war John resisted getting back into a grey flannel suit or any suit. He wanted the freedom to have color, style and different fabrics. For a while I thought he was going to pull it off. He would have been a good flower child. But look at the turn of civilization since Earth Day! I'm fully aware of what we've become. I'm beginning to see it very clearly in a small endeavor like Quiet Mountain with millions of acres of unsettled civilization around it, and the small amount which is left for settlement can quickly show the greed. And this time again the government is competing with its citizens.

"Then we did come West! A surprise to me! It was wild! We found and bought a part of Selene Mountain. We ran down the mountain sides in the dark not knowing what our footing or terrain was. We were so high nothing bothered us. In the dark we really didn't know where the county pavement was. If the terrain was down we knew we'd get down to the county road sooner or later. A nephew was with us. And we weren't all together. Each one was on their own running down the mountain in the dark.

"But I'll tell you we have never seen such beautiful mountain property within reach of the individual. This beautiful view within reach of individual ownership! National Forest land yes! But not what was in private ownership and so close to town! It was like an untouched garden! A garden of mountain surprises! A boulder here, there! A crevice between boulders that you could barely walk through. A boulder to climb. A flat boulder to lie on top nude and take in the sun way up there near the top sandstone rim. A beautiful fir. One that someone cut the top out of for Christmas the second winter we owned the property." Her voice fell. "A boulder that one mountain man-friend thought he'd like to blast out and carve a room to live in. We thought it would be fun too!" In Judith's mind her voice was singing a joy remembered,

in sadness felt, '*With someone like you, A pal*
so good and true, I'd like to leave it all
behind and go and find Someplace that's known
to God alone...' Why is it so wrong to have a
dream?"

"It's not wrong," he said.

"Since I was young I've dreamed of a house
on a hill with lots of trees and ground around
it. But to be honest I didn't dream big
enough to comprehend the Rockies. It was
definitely a more gentle mountain. But I'm
happy here. This is what I want it to feel
like."

"You did a good job. Quiet Mountain will
always be a masterpiece. When I saw this view
and all the Ponderosa pine and the space for
each homesite I knew this was it!"

"We were alone and didn't tell anyone for a
long time because we'd already been cornered

once when word got out but since we hadn't closed the deal we denied that we had purchased. We lived in a fantasy world of work and imagination. There are large boulders on the edge of that cliff north of my lot, we would lie on and hear Beaver Creek below in the spring run off. I have a picture of John on one. We named the boulders Stockade Point and imagined we were in a Western, hiding among the boulders and would shoot anyone coming up the mountain. John loved fantasy and always wanted to write fantasy."

"This is the time for me to read some of your writing. May I?"

She nodded yes. "I have a room at home as well as one set aside in the rear of the office. We'll go there after we finish eating."

The next time she saw Markham, he said, I read that story! Every word!" He looked at Judith anew. He made no other utterance. He looked stunned. "I would like to show this to someone I know. Do you have another copy?"

"Yes."

"I never expected this. Why don't you give more time to your writing? If I had your gift I'd go for it!"

"I don't know what kind of gift I have," she said.

"You are gifted!"

"But how did I do it? Can I do it again?"

"Of course you can! You've got something to work with! Why aren't you using your gifts?"

"It takes money! That's why John and I bought land and developed it—to have some money!"

"You went to a lot of trouble!"

259

"I know it now. But it needn't have been this way."

"Maybe."

CHAPTER 19

EGBERT'S DEATH

A drought covered a huge part of the continent. Most of Mexico, except the coastal regions, north from Mexico City up through the states—Texas, Arizona, Oklahoma, Kansas, Nebraska, the Dakotas, Colorado, Utah, Wyoming, Idaho, Eastern Oregon and Washington, California and into Canada.

In northern Mexico a picture of a rancher using a blow torch to burn needles off cacti so that his cattle could get moisture from the thick, fleshy cacti pads was on the front page. The environmentalists ridiculed his greed in the news. He should not be raising cattle but should be raising grain.

Pictures of young farm families, holding young children in their arms and standing in barren wheat fields, appeared on the front pages. One wheat farmer in Nebraska found one wheat seed that had germinated and was struggling for its life. He pulled the thin sprout loose and held it up for the news camera. Only one stem of wheat in his whole field had attempted to seed. Not only were domestic animals in trouble but wildlife was disappearing and dying.

Arthur Stahlek started a column in the local paper on the page the newspaper had turned over one day a week to the environmental news. The drought was getting so bad the paper asked someone in agriculture to write the column every other week. Art informed and reminded the readers that agriculture preserves open space, views, and, yes, wildlife. One full column addressed production figures in the local counties. We need the media, he wrote, local and national, to give us coverage and desist from giving more-then-equal coverage to opponents of agriculture and water storage. Irrigation feeds all types of wildlife. We need the project built, he wrote. The ponds are dry. Cattle will have to be sold. Cattle prices are brutally low. Naturally, feed prices are very high.

The mesa east and south of Quiet Mountain still had some irrigation from the dam further north but the ditch rider was having to say *No!* to many junior ditch users. "The sheriff's getting a lot of calls. I try to keep the peace but with the drought I'm staying out of it and I tell them it's a civil matter. I'm going to lock down the whole system. Too many people are trying to take water.

"And, no, no one dumped water out of the system last winter except Burbank opening six locks and running water for a month to restore pre-dam vegetation and pre-dam habitat. And that was in the papers. *There was a lack of snow. It's called a drought."*

In May, June, July and August there were dry lightning storms. A mix of cold and hot air and lightning with no rain. Fifty-nine forest fires burned in New Mexico in one week. One burned for a month in the mountains. In Arizona another burned for weeks and stopped at 57,000 acres before it could be extinguished. By late August there was a total of sixty forest fires in Arizona. There were many fires in Oregon. Fires burned east and south of Luna City. One north and another west. Smoke covered the sun for a good many days at the worst. Eyes ran tears from the prevailing smoke in the air.

The Hopi in Arizona prayed for water. Their dead cows did not have an odor because they had no moisture in their systems. They lay on the barren red earth their skeletons outlined under their hides. Five million acres burned in the West and it was not over. It was the third driest period in the century.

On his ranch Matt Stahlek had developed ponds for watering his cattle and other livestock. The wildlife partook of the water too. And up in the mountains on his National Forest lease Stahlek, like other lease holders, developed springs for watering their herds and the wildlife. Through their labors they acquired the lease and water rights adding to the equity of their operations. The bank had a lien on Stahlek's cattle. Stahlek hoped to sell this fall. Prices so low, he'll not get enough to pay off his bank loan. Matt went to the bank and told his problems and asked for an extension. The bank encouraged him to stand his ground. But before the papers were fixed the bank reviewed its accounts and leaned toward the winning rafters and their touristy clients.

Matt returned to his fields and his range. He saw that the cattle must be brought down to the river and he could no longer accommodate the rafters by using ponds which have gone dry. The cattle's lives were more important then the rafters. Before he could round them up he saw a cow off in a draw laying on its side. Instinctively he knew what had happened. This cow was to deliver soon. He went home and called Animal Damage Control. He went back to the cow which was still alive. The federal specialist arrived. The coyote ran. The federal specialist shot and killed it.

The calf was dead and partially eaten. The cow was paralyzed from fighting off coyotes and giving birth at the same time. Matt hoped the cow would recover and get on its feet again. The specialist pointed out bite and chew marks on the dead calf and areas eaten away from the cow's hind end as evidence coyotes did the damage. The cow finally had to be destroyed. The coyote lay on its side with its beautiful bushy tail extended like a show piece.

After the federal specialist left, Matt Stahlek finished walking his range. Walking the range, or the fence, or the irrigation ditch, before it was taken away, always hoping, taking the risk, that weather, rain, snow fall, the market, neither too much nor too little, will prevail in his favor and the crops and herds will produce. He felt good about what he did. He felt a part of the world community. He had no idea to whom his crops gave sustenance. Nor to the people of which country, nor how far his grains traveled. His face was weathered like old wood.

It had been a good community in which he had ranched. Neighborly. Willing to help one another. Lend a hand. Accept help when needed. It was this kind of community and behavior which did not protect him from harm now. It was this way of living which set him up for the first opening wedge of the rafters. It was their world and their habits of behavior that left Stahlek unprepared and susceptible to one shock after another. And left him immobilized while it built and built like a residual trama.

He heard the familiar rattle. It was right beside him. Coiled. With reflex action he pulled his revolver from its holster. His aim was good. The rattler relaxed its coil. Matt relaxed too in the comfort of knowing Ida, Ruby and Sullivan's wife, at the suggestion of Arthur, were taking marksman lessons at the local shooting range. They've had about a month of weekly lessons now. They felt a new security from this added skill. More and more people, women as well as men, were arming themselves.

There were many problems in the West today. More and more people felt intuitively that the environmentalists could be provoked into fighting the Indians. They did not seem to like the Indian. It was hard to come to this conclusion. But it was definitely felt. More and more the covetous, greedy, avaricious, selfish nature of the gungho environmentalist was becoming clear.

If the environmentalists fight the Indians over water, the non-greedy people could swing the battle. The big environmental movements have a diabolical plan—*Rid the earth of people!* So much concentrated greed! Insanity reigns! This was why it was easy to dismantle Western dams.

Stahlek rounded up his cattle to bring them down to the river bank for water. The rafters were trying to get one more tour loaded before the river got so low they had to quit for the season. On the Rio de los Luna below the face of Selene Mountain where Quiet Mountain was situated, river people slid rubber rafts into the stream. The trucks made tracks and beat down the riverside grass. The bank would soon be bare from traffic. A catamaran and kayak were nearby. The river to one-half its width belonged to Matt and Ida Stahlek. The river outfitters used Stahlek's bank for embarking without permission. Further downstream they disembarked on Sullivan's gentler slope. It was a three-hour trip in total time. A truck hauled the equipment back for an afternoon tour. A bus hauled the clients back to their respective hotels and motels. In the morning the river tours began after Stahlek's cattle had watered. In the late afternoon, the tours quit the river before the cattle, and later the deer, came to drink of the river.

Rafting is an entertainment industry, relaxing, like visiting a zoo, a cavern, a stage play. Most of the value, capital and wealth, created by the industry was in the manufacturing of the rafts, kayaks, ammo cans, ice boxes, float jackets, wearing apparel and other equipment much of which came from the extraction of minerals. Otherwise an industry was art, occupation, business. Human exertion employed for the creation of value, regarded by some as a species of capital or wealth and its labor. The rafters and the ranchers were on a collision of cultures.

The rafters were claiming dominant use of the river.

All users of the river disturb its waters—metropolitan use, embarking, disembarking, dragging equipment in and out of the river. There is a clean water act passed by congress but it was not being adhered to here nor enforced. If enforced one cannot even put a spade in the river water nor probably a rafting paddle. Stahlek had developed another pond early in the year to relieve the situation with the growing rafting trade. But now the pond was empty. The earth was cracked around its upper edges.

Stahlek had never given permission to the river outfitters for use of the river and bank. He was never asked. He had built the pond because the rafters had extended their day, now using the river and bank from early morning until sundown. They made four tours a day.

It was when the rafters usurped the river, that Stahlek had built one more pond. It had been difficult for the cattle to drink. The rafters didn't like the mooing cattle, and there were so many cattle. If Stahlek wasn't watching, the outfitters would stone the cattle. Stahlek had had the vet out for one cow. This evening with no water on the ranch it was imperative for Stahlek to address the problem. He hadn't done it because he and Ida didn't like to fight with the younger generation. It was too much like fighting with their son, Arthur, and wife, Ruby.

"Let the cattle drink," Stahlek said to the guide. "They'll get through and be through until morning."

"But we're under contract to give these people a tour and they have other things to do!"

Stahlek was sure it never occurred to the outfitters that he had a deed to the bank that extended to one-half the stream bed. He knew now he should have informed the outfitters early on. He had to do it now for his cattle's sake.

"You'll have to let the cattle drink or I'll have to not permit use of this river bank."

Stahlek felt tremulous after he finished. Something told him he shouldn't have to be talking this way.

"How can you do that! You don't own this river!"

"I own this bank and my land goes into half the river channel."

"That's an archaic law. It's not adequate for the times we're living in."

It became apparent the rafting outfitters never considered or thought of asking permission or to approach Stahlek for information and work out a purchase right to the river. No, their habits were to claim they were the dominant public users of the river and therein were their rights. And even with such a claim they were never able to pay anything for use of the river bank. Also with their people numbers they *were the greater good.* But not in cattle numbers. And this was the conflict.

The rafters called a meeting of the several rafting companies constituting sixty people counting all employees. They laid claim to an industry with gross income profits in the six figures, $192,000 versus fourteen millions gross income from ranching and agriculture. One member suggested they offer Stahlek lease money but this was shrugged off. "He wouldn't want to give up watering his cows."

"He doesn't have any other place to water them."

"Wonder what a fair price would be if we could work something out?"

"How much money do we have to work with?"

"Not much and the season won't be good this year. A short season."

"He'll sell cattle in the fall but that's too late for us."

"We've got dominant use on our side! What are we worried about?"

They ended the meeting feeling *comfortable* with dominant use. In a good season one company can easily introduce over 3,000 city people to rafting. The whole rafting industry in the area may be 30,000 people.

Stahlek's cattle were milling around. Stahlek had had too much. "I built a pond to accommodate you. The pond is now dry. The cattle will have to drink here. Morning and evening."

The rafters conferred. "I guess our schedule is messed up. The river is slow. That'll make us even later and slower each trip. Tell them at the office to cancel one tour."

All five hundred head of cattle took up the river bank.

"They're beautiful! So many. I've never seen a herd of cattle."

"When do they water in the morning?"

"About 6 a.m., Ma'am."

"Let's get up early and come back and watch them."

The outfitters got their clients to safety in the bus.

Stahlek with his dog, Mollie, kept the cattle moving and heading back to pasture.

But eventually, the rafters were like his cattle, too many to deal with. He tried driving his old pickup with a water tank to pull a lot of water for five hundred head of cattle.

The outfitters wrote letters to the editors of the local paper. To Stahlek's surprise he was reading that milk was bad for adults. Very bad. It had glue in it! Only good for infants. Nature never intended adults stay on milk. He learned red meat was even worse! And there was the point of discharge and the clean water act and news articles and grants and taxes for testing the belching of his cattle's effect upon the ozone. It was all mind boggling.

Then came the notice from Timber Management that his grazing fees would be raised dramatically and within another year be discontinued and the improvements he had made in the forest will be taken by Timber Management.

Then the letters to the editor gladly printed by the newspaper for their reader interest:

"The ranchers are lazy and not good managers or they'd have stored water before it became critical.

"It's not true that in the past all the rivers went dry. That's just heresay.

"The cattle shit on the river bank. We have to clean it up each morning. The towns south of here have contaminated sewage to drink. Cattle should be stopped from using river banks.

"The dairy co-op is a rip off. They charge five dollars for a membership.

"The overconsumption of nature's resources has resulted in having little or no water, which resulted in continually treating a symptom by feeding cactus to cattle. It is now known that man's extreme obsession with eating animals and their by-products has created many ecological problems that affect the health of every one."

And this letter was addressed to Matt Stahlek, himself:

"Yes, it does require a radical change to get you out of your vehicle to ride your bicycle. It does require a radical change to see how many dishes you can wash or showers you can take with the least amount of water. It does require a radical change to investigate new lifestyles that prioritize walking more lightly on our earth. It does require a radical approach to get people to explore their inner realms and increase self-awareness that includes both social and natural environments."

There were those letters psychologically constructing the Indian.

"It is ironic that the local Indian is so bent on disrupting the land and destroying a river. It is the antithesis of what the Native spirit has stood for.

"It is so different from the Lakota who continue to struggle to protect the Black Hills from destruction. I am dismayed. Can you convince me the draining of a river, the flooding of a basin, the destruction of habitat are all so necessary? Please search your hearts and walk in beauty."

It was these letters and the general excitement that attracted Egbert, Roland, Stan, Connie, Hubert, Jamie and Laurie to Stahlek's river bank. They were hired by the Washtub Rafters. Again the rafters were occupying the bank when Stahlek arrived with his cattle and dog, Mollie. Stahlek sat his horse, Prince, and watched. The rafters hurried but they couldn't push city people faster than was safe. A bull lunged suddenly from a stone thrown at it. The bull shook his head and horns angrily. Egbert laughed. "You're going to get sued, mixing your cattle with these tourists!"

"I didn't mix them," Stahlek said calmly. "I saw you stone that bull."

"You can't prove it!"

"Get out, all of you! I've taken enough!"

The raft owners were busy with clients. Stahlek dismounted, walked over and addressed them.

"You've come too early. These cattle have to drink. Your employee there has just driven a bull into that group of tourists. I can't afford to carry liability insurance. I make no profit from your operation. Take these people off my land!"

The raft owners took Stahlek seriously but Egbert knew no consequence of his acts. He stood laughing and jeering.

Stahlek was infuriated.

"Get off!"

While the raft owners were trying to decide what to do, Egbert called, "You haven't the guts to manage your land!" He laughed crazily.

Stahlek raised his gun and shot Egbert who didn't even see the gun. His head was thrown back and his eyes were closed with jeering laughter. The bullet went right through the head and split it open. The interior flew everywhere. Egbert jumped around his nervous system still going. The rafters and clients grabbed hold of him. His body was hard to handle with its jerking and rush of adrenaline. Finally Egbert collapsed and lay on the ground, the jerking subsiding as the blood rushed out.

"We have to leave. Get everyone into the van."

No one helped nor comforted Stahlek. He was weeping as he headed the cattle up the hill, a stooped, weary and broken man.

Tears made their way down his weather-worn face. He wiped them away with the back of his hand.

The deputies pulled up alongside him and showed their badges. Stahlek turned his pistol over to them and asked them to follow him to the ranch until the cattle were in.

In the ranch house, with deputies standing nearby, Matt told Ida, "I killed a rafter."

It took a while for Ida to comprehend. Then she put her arms around Matt but he couldn't give her comfort and pushed her away. Then he

clung to her. "They are worse than rustlers!"
He broke totally as she held him in her arms.
The deputies dealt kindly with Matt as they
lead him away.

CHAPTER 20

THE DAM BREAKS

Sometimes there were clouds and sometimes they looked promising but all year they'd been moving eastward where that part of the continent gets more rain than it can handle. More often there were no clouds at all. No promise. And when there were clouds the hot air of the region mixing with the cold upper air produced lightning. Daily there were lightning storms. Lightning without rain. Fires ignited and burned thousands of acres all over the West.

Las Vegas and Southern California wanted Colorado water badly. They used protecting Colorado's environment as a guise. The Sonora Club of California was heavy into the act, filing lawsuits every which way and more often against the federal government then corporations, small companies, and individuals. It was a cold civil war fought at the crucial federal government level.

The Department of Judicature suspended the 1988 water policy of the former Home Secretary now that the Pre-Columbian Act gave the Feds the water rights. The Feds were seeking to wrench control of water from the states and give primacy to the federal government. If so, the West loses.

The grazing reforms of higher fees and takeover of all improvements ranchers have made on their leases were a veiled attempt to grab water. The federal government may also regulate control of water through the Imperiled Species Act and the Pure Water Act. Every water right in the state was under serious threat. Colorado was vastly outnumbered in representation. Since the water was not for sale, the federal government in effect was stealing it. Water storage was a necessity in the arid West.

Worst of all the state's largest newspaper, newly owned by Easterners, joined the East, California and Las Vegas. *The Times* played into the hands of downstream developers, who rubbed their hands together gleefully when they read *The Times'* suggestion that the region shelve its large water projects and instead concentrate on sustaining "a growing river rafting industry." But now the river rafters had pulled out. Not enough water. A senator from the local region asked the paper, "Where was *The Times* when these powerful downstream interests opposed paying Indian tribes for water that presently flows down to these downstream interests free?"

The Home Secretary Burbank and Ecological Agency Administrator Christine White testified in the capitol before a liberal ecological task force.

Burbank, Harvard educated Westerner now turned against the West, in a wide pin striped suit, chewing nimbly on his pen, testified that budget cuts were impacting the environment and even public health.

Christine White's head tilted backwards, and her sleepy eyelids looked through low eye slits at the audience. She wore a deep V-neck, navy dress with large white buttons spaced far apart between white applique vertical stripes. The dress stretched up and up following her long, strong neck holding up a well-sculptured head which was adorned by a short bob with bangs, following around her ears, each ear showing off a modest earring.

She was corn-fed, tall, large, and well-proportioned. Imperial and could easily rule the universe if the liberal ecological task force could get the conservative leadership to stop circumventing the budget process. "We cannot ensure the American people their air is clean, their drinking water is safe, the health of their children is protected," White declared.

Burbank told the task force the conservatives were abusing the budget process, by inserting language in appropriation bills to "make radical changes in environmental laws that could not be enacted in regular bills. It's a frontal assault on the Imperiled Species Act done in the backroom process under guise of budget restraint," he said.

In the background of the task force speakers' table were other healthy imperial youths with earrings, nose rings and energetic smiles.

The conservative Representative from Alaska dismissed the task force hearing as a "media event, plain and simple". "It was an outright mockery of the system to conduct a media event for liberal congress people and invite liberal political appointees to attack conservatives," he said.

But this media event resulted in the President giving environmentalists "affected interest status", i.e. legal standing to challenge Timber Maintenance leases, thus inviting long and expensive litigation.

The Rio de los Luna was mysteriously rising although there had been no rain in the valley and no snow melt in the mountains. The water was not muddy but clear. The river had been increasing for the last three days.

Reclamation inspectors inspected the dam up in the mountains. They determined it was the dam producing the water but could not find the exact trouble. The dam was built in the Thirties to bring electric power to the region.

On the fourth day the breach in the dam broke wide open and the waters tumbled down to fall with a mighty force churning and tossing about the big boulders, flooding the canyon, rushing into the valley, spreading out over the valley floor up to the highway elevation and then over the highway itself.

People drove up to the mesas surrounding Luna City to view the flooding in the valley. It had been a decade since the last flood. There was much excitement. Horses, cattle and people must evacuate. The onlookers watched a small herd of horses left on a small flat island. Word went around, "They'll get to them. They're moving all the animals out to higher ground."

The water kept rising until it reached Broadway. It rose above the floors of the shops, cafes, and into the first floor and basement of the Grand Hotel. It rose until it reached Hardrock Mountain at the border of downtown, made a left and headed on south out of the city.

What was left were layers of mud. The local hardware store sold out of scoop shovels and more were ordered to get the downtown functioning. On the streets Jarvis' road graders, with Cameron supervising, bladed the mud into piles and loaders lifted it into city snow trucks to take the mud back to the Luna River or to whomever needed good soil. The debris from the stores, the unsalvageable, was piled up on the sidewalks. All had to be hauled to the dump. People came to look the piles over. Some found items they could use.

Robert Markham rented a suite from the Grand. He also rented storage space in the basement for film and scripts he was working on while spending the season in Luna City. He dreaded to think what he might find as he walked down the stairs to the basement. His film was stored on a high shelf right under the flooring. The scripts were lower. The water was held back somewhat by each wall. It had gotten pretty close to the rear of the hotel. Markham took the film up to his rooms. The scripts were soaked. He asked and obtained space to spread the sheets out for drying. He called his agent to obtain fresh scripts.

The bar of the hotel was not functioning. They were waiting for new carpeting which had to be ordered as the carpet store got inundated also. And, of course, they were still cleaning up.

Judith had driven down from Quiet Mountain where the earth was bone dry. She was amazed at the two worlds and wished it would rain a slow, steady rain to soak in good. She was making some notes in her Jeep when Markham stopped by.

"Let's go for a drive," he said. "What a mess! Let's get out of here. What direction do you want to go? North to the mountains or someplace south in the desert?"

Despite wanting to get away they were drawn north to the dam. They suspected criminal work. Robert had on his hip high rubber boots. He wanted to have a look at the dam.

"You might want to make some notes." They stopped by her apartment and she put on rubber boots."

Robert found a ledge along the dam wall to get to the center where the water had broken through. The lake was drained and the bottom very muddy. The Luna River, very narrow and drought ridden, ran in its old bed.

"I need to go where we can use the binoculars to examine the dam."

"Way up are people in the river. Before it rises against the levee we could walk down it too."

"Let's drive north and try following the river to where we can examine the dam."

They walked the river, treacherous and rough with so many stones, rocks and boulders emptied into it from the high mountains of the Continental Divide. But they were caught up

297

in the excitement too. It was amazing after fifty years that the old river bed was being used again.

Robert focused the binoculars and scanned the dam closely. "Black marks to the left of the breach!"

Judith adjusted the binoculars and found the black marks.

"Do you suppose the dam was dynamited?"

"I think we should read *Mother Green!* literature. We might learn something."

Robert shot a lot of pictures of the black spot and Judith made notes. They returned down the creek. "I never dreamed I'd run into all of this coming here to find a quiet place to work and for my breaks. I thought the West would be quiet."

"Not any more. It's being populated from the north, south, east and west. And there's not enough water to go around."

Back at the Grand, Markham showed Judith the enlargements of the eagle's feather and he explained how it was constructed in detail. He had taken large close-ups of all parts of the feather and the books told him how eagles fly and now he's to study how their eyes are constructed. He knew producers he might interest in a nature film on the eagle. And others he would make aware of what was taking place in the advance of populating the West.

Judith said John would like to see this. "John cared more about the wildlife and nature than about the development. I liked that about John but someone had to make it pay and that's where I came in."

"Yes," Robert said thoughtfully observing her.

"John most of all wanted to be a writer. But after that it wasn't clear what direction or purpose the writing was to take. He was extremely ambitious but needed more reality in his life. He got everyone around him writing, including Johnny and me. We wrote without formal training except living with John. I wonder now what will happen with John out of our lives."

"Good question," Markham said. He was still watching Judith. Judith was in a reverie and not bothered by Markham's eyes upon her.

"I would like to read more of your writing. I'm always interested in fresh new voices. I seem to have the time being hung up with eagles. I'd like to get my house going."

Judith, still remembering, nodded she knew.

"When I get this mess cleaned up why don't you give me some more material to read?"

"I will," she said knowing she couldn't makes sales of land either and she needed them badly.

"You're an interesting woman," Robert said. "It will be interesting to read what you write."

"Yes, I'll show you," she said. Looking at Markham directly, she said without passion, "Had you not had the experience with the eagles, I would not show you my writing. I don't think you would understand it."

Markham agreed. He got up and walked to the south bay window and looked south. Far in the distance he could see the mesas and mountains of New Mexico, Arizona and Utah. If they had dinner, they could talk more.

"I would love to have dinner with you," he said.

"Yes, let's," she answered.

CHAPTER 21

IDA RUNS THE RANCH

Up against a barbed wire fence with snow-covered mountains in the background a heifer lay resignedly on her stomach, with her bent front knees and hooves anchored on the earth, her back legs thrust forward, meeting the front hooves, her tail raised, her calf's head beginning to show in the birth canal, its front feet coming out close to each side of its head. Ida Stahlek had pulled a hard twist rope from its coil on the ground, one end she had wrapped around her down filled jacket, the other end she had fastened behind the calf's head. There was tension in Ida's bent knees and hips and the concentration she gave to the birthing was written all through her body. Ida pulled the rope taut helping the calf. Only its hips and rear feet were yet to be born.

303

With good luck the calf would be licked off by its mother and would be on its feet soon after delivery.

Ida ran the ranch, doing all the things she did with Matt when they were a young couple just starting out. Only now she was older, much older, and doing it alone. Next she would bring the herd to the river bank and later see what was left of her chickens.

Arthur had listed his parents ranch with Hurst. He wanted the ranch himself but the need to sell it had come too soon. Arthur and Ruby helped Ida and were on the lookout for hired help to be paid when the cattle or ranch were sold. There was room in the ranch house for a single worker and the bunk house could be cleaned for a couple. Only exceptional people liked ranch work any more.

Ida visited Matt in the county jail often. Matt felt the weight of guilt and of victim both. In his mind he was having difficulty separating them. When he got to feeling guilty, Ida would say, "Don't give sanctions to the rafters taking over our river bank. Our cattle must have water, far more than the rafters do!"

Matt worried about all the work Ida was left to do. "Have the heifers dropped their calves?"

Ida told Matt she had to help the blond one. She used her hard twist and the tractor as a brace to pull the calf and it's doing okay.

Matt winced. "Wasn't Arthur able to help?"

"He planned to but hadn't gotten back from bringing his sheep up from New Mexico when I found Blondie in labor and struggling. So I went home and started the tractor and drove it out to where she was and helped her. I didn't bring the calf inside as it looked plenty strong but I don't know if the heifers teats are long enough yet for the calf to suckle. I'll watch to see if it is nursing."

There was agony on Matt's face and his face had become drawn and worried. "I shouldn't be here. It shouldn't have happened this way."

"I know. But there is nothing we can do about that. Arthur has talked to Francine. I think Francine is going to represent you. I want him to. I'm hearing many things not good about that boy Egbert Easterly. It's possible he might have had something to do with the breach in the dam and who knows what else. We are going to help you, Matt."

The relationship between Steve and Jim Murray had changed. Of course Steve would not be participating in the on-going timber cutting protests but he still wanted Jim for a friend. But Jim was confused.

"I'm still a protestor," he said. "I do think someone has gotten something screwed up but I don't know enough to know who. I'm just not ready to quit. I may not protest this cutting because I know your father and I know he doesn't fit the category they're talking about. I just have to watch and think. I know I don't want to join the group that Egbert belonged to. God!"

"There are other things. I've decided not to return to Atlantic League. I'm through with their garbledegook. I'll go locally to Indian-Anglo and I'll hear the same left leaning tower gook in all my political science courses but I'll have my dad to play it against.

307

"Also I've talked to Ms. Carver. I've heard her troubles with Egbert's mother and Darth Damuel and all their crowd. She's resigned from her contract to teach and is opening a private school. Jim, it's a tough job teaching anything unbiased today.

You got to be destroying this country or else. She's acquiring students and I've signed on to help her. My dad and mother and the Camerons congratulated me. She could use more help. Come!"

"I will honestly think about it. I wish I had a father like yours."

"Why don't you talk to your father?"

"I have two fathers. A natural and a step. My step father and mother and I go fishing together. My real dad is the one to talk to but he's always busy. Overseas, etcetera."

"Then come. My dad will talk to you. I just know he will!"

"You talk to your dad first. I have to get my feelings straight before I talk with anyone."

"He'll help you."

"Not if you're as mixed up as I am."

CHAPTER 22
JUDITH AND HER BILLS

Judith had left the Luna City Bank with no good news. Her problem was how to keep Quiet Mountain between now and the next sale, whenever that would come, after the building moratorium was lifted in another six months, if the Planning Department didn't come up with something new, what with all the influx of people that made this high, dry outdoors-air-conditioned country extremely popular in which to live.

She was irritated with the bank and wanted to do her finance figuring someplace besides the bank's parking lot. Her downtown office was not yet renovated after the flood and now there was a shortage of office space downtown in which to find the right place to move. Her rental home offered no inspiration. Almost in defiance she backed out of the bank's parking lot and decided to go up to Quiet Mountain and live the dream of John's and hers, peace and all the other good things that Quiet Mountain was to provide for them—the writing time, the friends, travel, all the dreams of later retirement.

Quiet Mountain was quiet when she arrived. She parked her Jeep on the lot she and John had chosen and got out, looked at the Moctezuma Range and the snows left from the winter, climbed out on a promontory and looked at the smooth green valley with a sprinkling of houses, and one new house built below her lot. Then she took a walk along the trail to the south, cut among the gamble oak and Ponderosa Pine. It was a lovely wooded walk. She hadn't taken anyone on a walk on Selene Mountain in a long time.

She wondered if Robert was still in town. She was sure he'd like to walk on up Selene Mountain and just discover.

When she returned to her Jeep she got her mail, a notepad and a folding chair and went over to the empty TV spool now a table to work on bills. There would be one lonely life policy of $10,000 from John's Navy Service, a term policy they couldn't cash and use for Quiet Mountain until his death; a $250.00 burial amount from Social Security, and his last month's pay. She was waiting to see what his retirement and Social Security figures for her widowhood would amount to. She looked at credit card allowances and interest rates which were still high from the early eighties. And she totalled the balances owed. She looked at her insurance earnings and estimated her time to be spent on insurance writing and

results.   It   was   a   very   tight   squeeze.   It
left   no   time   for   mistakes,   play,   nor   other
ventures.   It   would   require   a   lot   of   faith,
prayer   and   moving   ahead,   winning   each   battle
as   they   came.

With   that   wrapped   up   and   some   order   and   plan
established   she   lay   down   on   the   shaped   boulder
beside   the   table   and   remembered   how   wonderful
it   was   lying   on   that   boulder,   any   boulder,
looking   through   the   pine   branches   at   the   blue
sky   and   white   cumulus   clouds.   She   felt   the
ecstasy   from   the   glint   of   the   sun   on   the   pine
needles   turning   in   the   gentle   breeze.   The
branch   swaying   back   and   forth   like   the   rocking
of   a   cradle.   The   breeze   had   the   same   effect
on   her   skin.   Heavenly.   It   was   4 p.m. and   the
hawks   were   circling   in   pairs   on   an   upper
current   of   air,   hunting   their   dinners.   John
and   I   knew   we'd   be   here   until   sundown,

figuring all this out to eventually become **Quiet Mountain.** There was no hurry and we were alone with out great secret. It was a time—we were only vaguely conscious of—something we hadn't quite experienced before. Time and more time just on and on. And every day a new discovery on Selene Mountain.

She ended her memory realizing she was now on her own. It was a strange feeling, this alone feeling. Each step she decided was it, alone. Then sadly came the words to a childhood song from the mythical west, from her growing up in Western Oklahoma.

"With Someone like you, A pal so good and true, I'd like to leave it all behind and go and find someplace that's known to God alone, just a spot to call our own..." and then she couldn't sing it even softly, and ended with

the question WHY? WHY? Why did it have to happen?

She drove back down to put pen to paper and to checks and carry on. The eagles were coming in from their hunt to their nest on Markham's lot. She parked and got out to watch them. A helicopter was hovering overhead making its customary count of eagles in the Beaver Creek area. There was something, a small animal spotted and one of the eagles made a sudden swift dive for it. The copter was zooming low to look into the tree tops. The speed of the eagle's dive intercepted the copter and cut the eagle in half. It fell as swift as the force of gravity to the earth. The first eagle took off in a hurry and made large circles over its mate's two pieces. It was very disturbed and seemed to darken the sky with its constant

315

circling. The helicopter settled on the Quiet Mountain road and the pilot joined Judith in watching. The eagle's seven foot wing span kept Judith and the helicopter pilot away from the fallen eagle.

"I've got to report it," he said.

"I don't think anyone is going to get near very soon," Judith replied. "I'm going to leave it by itself for now." She knew she would come again at nightfall and see how the surviving one was doing.

Watson's wife came to the road to see what had happened. She complained the helicopter was dangerously close to the nest. "At what point does it become harassment?" she asked.

"I was at 200 feet. We go down that low just to verify there is an eagle in the nest. We are not trying to count eggs or enumerate eaglets once they're hatched. It's hard to find the eagle. They get camouflaged with branches, green or dried leaves. Easier to find their large nests. It helps if they're on a snag. Otherwise, if you just take a picture it takes much enlarging to find the eagles. The bureau is not required to obtain any type of permit."

"I just know that as a person, if I were lying out and had a helicopter hovering over me, the wind and noise would be terribly frightening."

"There have been reported instances of adult eagles attacking aircraft," the pilot said.

"I guess I feel that with so many government agencies, we citizens need to make sure that we are bird-dogging them. We need to let them know we are watching them and don't expect them to overstep their bounds. That helicopter was hovering dangerously close to that nest!"

Judith drove up to Quiet Mountain at night. She was not certain she could view the dead eagle. That is, she was not certain of its mate who might be vicious. But she would ascertain the situation and proceed cautiously. If she was not able to view the deceased, she would enjoy the millions/billions of stars at night up on the mountain. She knew she'd be there if John were alive. But he isn't and she'll have to learn to do things alone.

Despite all the trouble, the dream of perfect life on a mountain came back in full force driving along Beaver Creek Canyon Road. The sky was clear. The stars would be magnificent. As she drove up Selene Mountain she began to think of Lot 21, wondering if Robert had heard of the accident. She had made the fourth curve in the climb up to her lot and parked on Quiet Mountain Road. Another car was also there. She walked up the hiking/horseback trail that would also be used for the water line—as soon as Damuel's protests and his influence allowed more work to be done. That wait, along with John's death and his salary ending, and no sales to be made with Damuel's pending lawsuit, made life difficult. She brought her flashlight to walk through the small gamble oak, mountain mahogany, service berry and other mountain woods and bushes to the protected clearing large enough for a large dwelling on Lot 21. The accident, she was sure, happened nearer the old tall snag to the north. As she came out of the protected clearing there was the eagle on the ground and Robert Markham taking its picture.

"Hi!" he said surprised.

She was sure he had not realized the many times she, John, Johnny, nephews and nieces had come to Quiet Mountain at night or even explored it at night before the purchasing of it.

"I was here when the copter was reconnoitering. He was very close. I was underneath the copter taking a picture. The copter had just moved over me when the eagle crashed. I got a picture of it. I'm sure Damuel will make something of this so I have a picture to protect myself."

Judith nodded appreciatively. "Has the mate disappeared?" she asked.

"It's been here. I stayed back out of sight. It's at a loss. Seems to take off and come back. It's been away quite a little while since dark. Keep your eyes out for the mate. Your flashlight? Turn it off.

"Look it's been cut in half. When you came I was wondering what the remaining mate would do. Will it have to find a widow or widower, or a younger eagle, or remain single. Birds mate for a lifetime you know."

"No, I didn't. I haven't been studying eagles as you have. Maybe you will find the answer in some of the books you're reading. Let me know. I was down on the road when the accident happened. The pilot has to report it, he said."

"Let's leave because the mate may return."

"Come with me to the lot John and I had saved. We've cleared an area in it and it just opens up. You'll be amazed. I was here this afternoon sorting bills and paying some.

Preferred to do it here rather than the bank parking lot."

"How's the bank treating you?"

"Not good."

The clearing was a complete surprise. There was the spool table with the folding chairs around it.

"Let's sit for a while."

"I like this!"

"Up in the woods in the dark!" she said gaily. "Your lot will surprise you too!"

Markham looked at Judith. "I'll bet you have a lot to write about with all this experience in the mountains."

"And you too! Let me read your notes. Those that go with your pictures. I'll bet that for me it will be an entirely new experience."

Markham said yes with smile.

"Have you ever experienced anything like this?" she asked.

"Yes and no. I envy you. It must have been wonderful to have this all to yourselves! When I speak of a place to get away this is what I mean. And I keep expecting to be happy."

"Me too."

"I tried Aspen after my wife died."

"How?"

"In a pedestrian-auto accident. She had been to her dressmaker getting ready for a trip, a grand one, overseas. Her mind was on it. A car passed her and she kept following it instead of watching the rest of the traffic. She stepped off the curb, was hit and died instantly. It was something! I wasn't expecting her to die any more than you expected John to die the way he did. We had

323

planned to find a second home, quiet, where I could work in off time. I tried Aspen winter and summer. I like the diversity here. In Aspen you're always in Hollywood. I found myself riding the ski lifts alone and there's so much faking. I'd make conversation with the other occupant by telling outrageous stories of my importance, what I did. I found it easy to impress the fakes. So I decided to get away from that. I searched and found Quiet Mountain on my own.

"In that home I'm going to build—someday—I want a wall in it that will be the focus of my home entertainment system. I've designed around the wall, plus music and piano, and will place the technical components in specially concealed places to receive the maximum audio and visual effects.

"A wall with depth and resolution that is more real than reality itself. Sound strategically placed to achieve **surround around sound.** I have such a wall in California. I'd like you to see it."

"I would love to see it. And I'd like to see it built on Quiet Mountain."

"I'm working on interactive films, where you push a button on a small remote control and create alternate versions of the movie you're viewing. I would like to make a regional filmmaking center here or have an office in some nearby city with high tech facilities that can make commercially viable films because I think we're on the verge with all this technology to be really ready for it plus brain food and it's beginning already—smaller, smaller, more personal films. For that market we're going to need screen writers. You can't do anything without a scipt."

    "I believe that and I'm ready for brain food in what we see and read."

CHAPTER 23

THE FIRE!

The column was way off to the northwest of Luna City, near the river, rising blackish and holding its shape for a good 200 feet high before the wind began to mushroom and spread it grayish with more smoke rising and joining the funnel.

A week or several days earlier it had been a very small fire that only a nearby neighbor, Hurst, who lived along Beaver Creek in the valley below Selene Mountain, could see. But Hurst and family were packed and ready for a vacation. He was sure someone would notify Timber Maintenance. After a few days more it became noticeable from the road and Francine saw it Monday morning driving along Beaver Creek County Road to his office in Luna City. He almost stopped, thinking he could take his army shovel in the trunk of his car, hike up the hill and knock it out but he was due in court at 9 a.m. and had a last minute polishing of his presentation. He could not afford to enter court half prepared. His client was depending on him heavily. So he drove on by, firmly believing someone in the neighborhood would take their time, especially in such a dry season. The timber covering the mountains had only 8% moisture content. The logs, Jarvis was cutting were light in weight and kiln dry, ready for use in construction.

When Francine returned home after a day in court he had forgotten about the blaze he had noticed in the morning. By the time Hurst returned home the column of smoke had turned into a wide expanse of fire covering a good acre of hillside. Hurst immediately joined the other callers to the Department of Timber

Maintenance. To his amazement the young woman fielding the callers said, "We're letting nature restore itself."

"If the wind doesn't blow it back on me!" Hurst exclaimed. "I'm right next to your land!"

"You'll be all right," she assured in a breathy, sexy voice.

Hurst watched the fire spread. It was now too large for one person to control.

He called the city fire department. Yes, they've been watching it and have wanted to help but have not been allowed up there. "The nationals tell us we're just local fire fighters and it's too inaccessible and too dangerous for city fire fighters without sophisticated resources. We'll offer again."

After three days of complaints from residents who feared unpredictable winds could push flames into their subdivision, fifty-two fire fighters and helicopter crews were assigned to the fire and all neighboring fire districts were there to help.

At first the fire followed the Timber Maintenance computer models which showed the worst-case scenario would char no more than a few acres all within wilderness. But then the fire took a design of its own. The fire moved eastward. As it got closer to the steep east side of Selene Mountain, it became a fearful threatening monster and continued around Selene Mountain and entered the outskirts of the city. A southeast wind changed the fire's direction and it moved closer to Rio de Los Luna River.

It burned dry weeds along the river's bank, then a strong gust blew some of the sparks over to Mercedes Island in the middle of the

river and started a blaze immediately. The
southeast wind continued and the fire's sparks
moved the fire from Mercedes Island over the
drought ridden, trickling stream of Luna River
onto the farther bank and onto the foothills
of dry oak brush of the larger Luna Mountain.
Now it would have a big mountain to feed on.

In the night the southeast wind gave way to
a wind from the north and the wind picked up
the Selene Mountain fire, made it brighter and
hotter, traveling southward towards the north
end of Luna City proper. When it rounded the
steep east bank of Selene Mountain it
threatened mountainside homes, snatching one
and threatening others. It arrived in
downtown Luna City with people helplessly
watching as nightfall came. By morning it was
raging down Broadway with helicopters
overhead. It entered the rear of the Grand

Hotel. Hendricks was at the desk calling all his guests. He'd sent messengers and employees to every one of the fifty rooms. He was on the phone, making sure everyone was out, when the heavy mahogany canopy over the reception desk collapsed and struck him atop the head, killing him instantly. Markham escaped to the front sidewalk with other hotel guests. The fire spread next door to the candlestick makers niche, took it quickly, then moved onto the Quiet Mountain offices. Judith was loading files when Markham came and advised her to stop and get out. She left with him. The county offices were gutted as well as the Luna City National Bank. Thereafter it was all wood, one building connected to the next with common walls.

It caught people asleep in their beds. Some did not make it, overcome by smoke. Tourists

were caught, not so much in the brick Grand as
in the wooden Colonel Walton House built a
year after the Grand in the last of the 1800s.
It was blistering hot out on the streets with
flames everywhere and through this the
prisoners were moved from the Luna County jail
including Matt Stahlek. Matt's health had
fallen with his imprisonment. He caught a
glimpse of the fire, heard the roar and felt
the heat as he was driven to the hospital with
heart pain. They put him on a respirator and
called for Ida and Arthur. Arthur was busy
with the fire. Ida came as quickly as
possible but Matt could not wait for her and
was gone when she arrived.

She fell across him weeping and asking him
not to leave her. The shock of no response was
more than she had ever imagined. The doctor
comforted her and a nurse took her to the

chapel in the hospital for prayer and to be with her.

"My son is working in the fire," Ida said. "Do not call him now."

In the residential section fire was so intense it was jumping across streets and devouring as if it knew no satisfaction. The intense heat created wind which kept blowing it further and further. The reservoir was empty from the breaching. The most important use of the water was for the fire. Everyone, but Frankel and Tom Gerry, who had come back to town to help protest the salvage logging contract Timber Maintenance awarded the Jarvis Logging Company, prayed for rain, rain and more rain. Finally, after more fire fighters arrived enough homes were foamed to retard and then stop the monster. Only city trees and other plantings remained for the fire to eat.

But Mother Green! raised her voice and threatened to sue Timber Maintenance for not constraining air pollution. Mother Green! cited laws prohibiting skies full of smoke and a lawsuit because prescribed burns had gotten out of control in the Maintenance control of the fire. Mother Green! cited wilderness laws that banned mechanical devices needed to create firebreaks in preparation for prescribed burning. Mother Green! and her followers were savage in their opposition to the citizens fighting the fire. They paid no attention to the risk endangered species were in not to mention people and their homes and lives.

Markham walked up the burned out part of Big Luna Mountain. The Hot Shots were ahead of him with fires closing in around them. They

335

were deploying aluminum sided fire shelters. He went back down.

For two hours the nine firefighters withstood noise, intense heat and flying cinders. The fire made three different runs on the right side of them. Inside the shelters it heated up to 110 degrees. During the hottest run there were glowing fire brands blowing into the shelters. They could hear large trees fall. The shelters were hell but did save their lives.

Finally the racket subdued and the Hot Shots were able to crawl out of the shelters. They walked to the burned out area where Markham had been. They could look down the mountain and watch the two helicopters taking turns filling buckets from Beaver Lake and taking off to dump the water on burning trees. They looked like they were doing a sky ballet, circling, waiting their turn to dip into the lake, loading, taking off to drop water on the fire. It was an amazing choreography. Pinpointing one tree at a time while a Hot Shot chopped down one tree at a time was slow business.

The Hot Shots walked to town and stopped at the nearest restaurant to get something to eat which was Mamie's and Jim's. Soon there was a crowd of hero worshippers around them and the local news *Luna Times* and radio heard their story. Later when Markham arrived and the Hot Shots learned he produced films, they talked freely of the adrenaline rush a fire like this gave them. "It's the thrill and excitement! The chance to work in so many areas of the U.S.," said Bob Eubanks, the 36-year-old supervisor of the Idaho crew. "How many fires have we worked together in the last five years?"

"I would say fifteen right off."

"And it hasn't gotten old yet. Every fire is different."

"It makes you feel good to know you've saved some trees and people's homes."

"You have interesting lives," Markham said. "I've never been around a raging forest fire before."

Bob Eubanks said, "If you're in an aluminum-sided shelter and you stop sweating your body has been pushed to the limit. You'll experience unbearable pain before collapse. You'll begin to panic just before losing consciousness." He noticed that a woman, Judith, had joined the party and was taking down what he said. "At this point your body is thermally stressed, and water becomes distasteful, especially if the water is warm. If water starts to taste bad or causes you slight nausea, try to drink all the water you have, since it will become very difficult to drink later."

"Let me have a picture of you guys."

They started acting for Robert. Jimmy grabbed Bob around the neck and started smooching him. Bob grinned and looked squarely at the camera lens. The others laughed. They hadn't had their pictures taken in this fire yet. In the morning they were expected to labor all day above the fire—a hazardous locale—to finish containment.

In the night, cool air began flowing down Selene Mountain Westward. James Burns, Moctezuma Timber Commander, switched firefighters' attention to Quiet Mountain. In

339

the morning, Laguna County Sheriff Richardson's deputies advised families to evacuate voluntarily. Beaver Creek County Road was closed to all except residents and officials. Jarvis and Cameron and their crews had left their logging and were bulldozing fire breaks and men were gouging out containment lines by hand around Quiet Mountain homes. The district fire chief had ordered Moctezuma Electric Company to turn off power in the area for a safety precaution. Many firefighters and trucks were under power lines while hosing the front lines with trucked-in water. Nighttime brought calmed and dying winds and cooler temperatures. Easterly winds then picked up and prevented the fire from spreading to Quiet Mountain where about seven or eight homes stood amid dry brush and trees.

Up on Big Luna Mountain air tankers and slurry bombers were dropping fire retardant on unburned trees and brush. Jarvis, Cameron, Steve and crew were now cutting fire breaks on Big Luna. The nine Idaho Hot Shots had been taken up by helicopter and released to begin chopping and containing. Robert Markham caught a ride up with Barney, one of the copter pilots, to see the extent of the fire. Surveying the scene, he saw Bob Eubanks and his crew walking up the mountain. Then he saw the glint of silvery survival shelters in the flames and smoke of Big Luna Mountain and knew instantly that the Hot Shots were in trouble. Barney, who had been a Smoke Jumper, also knew. There was a wall of flame 150 feet high that just exploded behind the Hot Shots.

The nine didn't make it into their shelters and perished in less than a minute after the fire trapped them.

Barney said, "The fire down there is so hot, probably 2000 degrees, that their lungs basically give out in a matter of seconds."

It happened so fast. The roar of the copter and the fire made shouting impossible. "Can't we phone? Can't we do something?" Robert Markham asked anxiously.

"Only Eubanks and his assistant have radios. They're blinded from each other. There is no visibility. At least they each should have a radio to know what the other can see but they don't."

The 150 foot wall of flame raced up the mountain at nearly 20 miles per hour enveloping the Hot Shots in swirling, choking smoke, and searing heat. Barney estimated again that the fire where it overtook the Hot Shots to be as hot as 2000 degrees. "Officially they'll list it as asphyxiation. Shall I circle around for a picture?"

"No!" Robert shook his head. "I can't! I didn't expect this. Let's go back. You'll know how to report it. I had dinner with them last night."

CHAPTER 24
AFTER THE FIRE

Markham left the copter, got into his car, and drove to Judith's, his body flooded with adrenaline. He was hardly aware of where or to whom he was going. He just knew he had to talk to someone. There was no way he could put his mind to anything else just now. His breathing was tight, his mind whirling. Nothing could be done for the Hot Shots. Nothing but to pray and wait for his inner storm to calm.

When he found Judith and told her, he said, "Let's do a good story on them. There's a lot to tell. You and I know that."

Yes, she agreed.

Afterwards Barney circled the other side of the fire where the heavy equipment and fire

344

fighters were cutting containment areas. The fire that exploded and took the nine Hot Shots was advancing. The crew was trying to enlarge the containment area because of fire crowning from tree to tree. Big trees just exploded in the intense heat of the fire. Jarvis and Cameron were bulldozing wide fire lanes. Steve was helping chop down trees. "This fire will burn until the snows fall," he said.

Suddenly a blackened tall pine toppled and Steve was in its path. He was right in line of the crashing timber. Barney settled the copter and got the body and brought it back to Luna City. Then circled back to tell Elmer Jarvis. Elmer gave an arm motion to Dennis Cameron. Cameron cut his motor and came over. "Steve is gone. Barney has taken his body to the hospital. What shall I do?"

"Go!" said Cameron. "I'll find someone to take your dozer."

There were still scooped up piles of rubbish left from clearing the flood dammage along Broadway. The fire burned more of these piles. As the Jarvis crew with Cameron taking over, and other backhoe and crane operators dug into fallen buildings, they found more bodies. Some the fatality to falling timbers or collapsed walls, blocked doors and suffocation. A gas explosion yielded three in one house. They found ten teachers from Kansas in the Colonel Walton House dead from suffocation before fire distroyed the hotel. The teachers had been on a tour of Indian Ruins, the high mountains and other scenery.

The nine Hot Shot bodies were in a makeshift mortuary. They would be returned to their homes and the teachers to Kansas. The eleven locals would all be buried in a special section being added to the Luna City Cemetery and dedicated to them as victims of the fire. The cemetery was a beautiful, peaceful setting on a gentle slope overlooking Luna City. The cemetery was in need of expansion and the fire made the expansion its time to come. The only way to expand was farther up the mountain as both the north and south ends of the cemetery were butting up against housing developments or canyons.

This brought the attention of the backpacking crowd who had also wanted the upper part of the mountain as a connecting point between the city and Beaver Creek Canyon to the Beaver Creek Trail Head. They had once asked for the cemetery and the bodies to be moved to another site. Now they felt the fire had brought the matter to a head and they asked that the fire victims not be put farther up the mountain. The cemetery association had no other place to expand and they had an option on the land to annex it and the association would not back down. The backpackers claimed hikers from all over the country. They wanted the land deeded to them for their connecting trail.

Frankel and Gerry were still in town awaiting the logging protest and were in protest mode. They encouragaed the hikers to insist on their trail. Burbank was coming to Luna City to show respect for the people damaged by the fire and especially to address the sacrifice of the nine Hot Shots' lives. Christine White was arriving with Burbank to be sure what water was left was pure and drinkable and check on any harm from air pollution.

The relatives of the victims were in no mood for negotiation. They wanted their dead buried and their grieving to heal. The clean-up crew was burning the rubbish along the river bank spreading the ashes where fertile soil was needed. That's why White had conme to town for the question of air pollution.

Markham had sent his pictures to the Associated Press along with Judith's description of the poor equipment the Hot Shots and Heat Seekers had—only bandannas for masks, no insurance, pay only for hours worked close to minimum wage. Luna City was getting a lot of attention.

Darth Damuel had asked for a special hearing on his expulsion from the school grounds. The cemetery question was also put on the special hearing.   The Sonora Club backed the hikers and had a meeting on what to do about the expansion of the cemetery.   They argued amongst themselves.   The members were adamant that the Luna Cemetery should not be expanded and, if not, what to do with the eleven bodies with no cemetery.

"Let them rot!" said a new face from California.   "That's how we handled the goats on Santa Cruz Island.   "It's a natural process!"

"The people won't allow it.   They'll find their relative or friends and bury them. Somewhere.   And they'll keep fighting for a cemetery.   I say crush the bones to quarter inch and spread for fertilizer.   If people don't want the fertilizer give it to the Park Service.   It will be like offering your vital organs to save others' lives. Very unselfish!"

The hikers protested any kind of burial—rotting, pulverized, or in the ground. They didn't want burials near their nature paths. They appealed to the Sonora Club to prevail in their favor. The Sonora Club had a direct line to Burbank and asked for his help. Burbank promised to find another solution. However, he did think that returning the bones to Mother Earth in a pulverized manner and planting a rose garden on top would meet with everyone's approval. The dead will only return to earth anyway, he reasoned, and the rose garden would make a beautiful memorial to the fire victims and something for the living to enjoy.

At the special hearing, Darth Damuel's trouble with the school administration was heard first. The school administration was seated on the podium. The principal of the district's grade school in the city came to the microphone and told the school board that Mr. Damuel was expelled from the school grounds because of verbal abuse to the teachers and also being a danger to others with his car and his impatience. "Mr. Damuel denies this but we have teachers her to speak otherwise. I'll call Ms. Carver first. Tell us, Ms. Carver, your experience with Mr. Damuel."

Alene Carver walked to the mike. "Yes, Mr. Damuel is abusive. He cursed me because I didn't and couldn't hang up on a parent and tend to his request. This is not at all unusual for Mr. Damuel. But he went further on April 24th of this year and used his automobile to harass and intimidate. He would bump into me while I was helping the children board the bus. This was frightening and dangerous. It was very difficult to perform my duties."

Three other teachers testified to similar experience with Mr. Damuel. The expulsion was upheld. Mr. Damuel was not happy.

Then the city council seated themselves and heard the arguments against the expansion of the cemetery. Attorney for the Sonora Club, Julie Baker, gave a report of how the problem of non-native goats on Santa Cruz Island off the coast of California, about 2,000 of them was handled. They were shot and left to nature. She horrified the bereaved. To assuage their grief she told them "we are all non-natives!" She focused on Rabbit Run, "Even the Indian! We are all intruders upon the planet and its natural inhabitents."

"Who do you hold responsible for putting us on this planet?" asked Robert Markham.

Baker avoided answering but suggested another option favored today—leaving one's organs for the benefit of others. That is too late for these departed but if we let the bones dry and then run them through a rock crusher to a small quarter-inch size and spread them on a new plat and plant it with roses it would make a beautiful memorial. It would be like leaving yourself for others' benefit."

"Not on our hiking trail or near it! We don't want to ride in an area like that!" said a hiker from Vermont.

At the hearing the hikers remained steadfast in their request for a nature path. They didn't want any thing like a cemetery no matter how beautiful, beside their hiking nature trail.

Mrs. Easterly said if the price was right she would use the fertilizer in her flower garden. She got enough angry glares from the bereaved to tone down her input.

Judith said, "I don't know how we ever got to a place of such absurdity but a vote ought to settle the question of the cemetery expansion. Why don't you, the council, call for a vote?"

"That might be one way but a lot of people here don't have a vote," informed Professor Albert Brown.

"What do you mean?" she asked. "Most in this room live here."

"But most people, especially those outside the city, don't have a vote."

"The city is in the county and both city and county are buried in the cemetery."

"But most didn't sign up with the government to manage their land and not doing so lost their vote."

"What are you talking about?" Cameron asked.

"This came about with Executive Order 126," Professor Brown said smugly.

There was mental bedlam in the sounds coming from his hearers. "How do you know such a thing? It wasn't in the papers!"

"Oh it was! In the legal classifieds. It's the law all right."

"Then we don't pay taxes!" another voice called out.

Taxes was not addressed," Brown said. "There will be changes." Brown looked at Judith. "Quiet Mountain is now an eagle preserve."

Markham took a picture of Brown's gleeful face. "You're talking about my land!" he told Brown.

"And mine! And mine! And mine!" went around the room and the bereaved and the land owners walked out enmasse. The sheriff found himself surrounded by angry citizens. He also had not heard of Executive Order 126. Sheriff Sherman agreed to take Deputy Jones and meet Burbank and White at the airport and hold them in custody. Arthur Stahlek, Robert Markham and Dennis Cameron followed for support.

The law returned with White and Burbank to the cemetery to show them where the graves will be dug for the eleven dead. Hank Burbank balked. "I am the Home Secretary!" The citizens voiced "No!" "How dare you?" Burbank confronted them.

The citizens were of one mind. "We want White and Burbank to dig the graves."

"That's out of our realm of duties. We need to consult the president!"

The citizens shouted, "Deputize anyone else needed to get the graves dug." Cameron and Markham were deputized. Gerry, Frankel, Professor Brown and Mrs. Easterly arrived. Sheriff Sherman had leg irons for the six. At the point of four gun-bearing lawmen at the ready, they obliged the sheriff and all six were in leg irons and each given a shovel.

The cemetery caretaker quickly measured off eleven plats and the shovelers were set to work with guns on them. The mortuary kept unloading the coffins of Hendrix, Steve Jarvis, Matt Stahlek, and the eight other locals lost in the fire. Pall bearers had already been chosen and they carried the coffins to the grave the relatives had chosen.

James Murray had been to the hearing, the first community public meeting he had ever attended. He was more lost in his own problems than those of others. He couldn't blame Steve's father. He couldn't blame the forest which was only renewing itself. He could not imagine crushing human bones just because there wasn't a place in Colorado to bury a loved one. And now with Steve's death there would never be a reconciliation. James was beginning to question the course he had pursured and it depressed him very much. There was uncertainty and doubt. He did not want to join Egbert's group or those like them. By early raising he was a builder not a destroyer. The appeal for James was for the good of the whole, civilization, not for the greed and gain that was so attractive to the action-hungry followers of the environmental movement.

James walked up the gentle slope of the cemetery to be with the others. Maybe say something condoling to Elmer and Joyce Jarvis and Ms. Alene Carver. They had all, like he, lost someone important to them. He could surely use their condolences too. He could see there was a large crowd on up and a hearse just passed by. He saw the Jarvises at a distance. Arriving closer, looking for direction, he couldn't cope with what he was seeing.

He closed his eyes. Looked again. There was Hank Burbank and Christine White, the Secretary of the Department of the Environment, in leg irons, shovels in hands, digging Steve's grave in the new annexation of

Luna Cemetery with the County Sheriff and three deputies surveiling them. James felt utterly betrayed. Utterly humiliated. Without thinking he pulled the revolver from the sheriff's holster and in quick succession fired shots killing both Burbank and White. Judith felt relief. She hated that she felt relief at murder but she had heard the rumor that all of Quiet Mountain was going to be listed a Stress Area and taken from her.

Now the diggers had two more graves to dig like in the Old West on the spot without elaborate preparation. It was good for the citizens to vent rage.

Frankel and Gerry refused. Both had good jobs awaiting them. Frankel in a large corporation and Gerry with a large environmental group. Sherman ordered, "Shovel!"

Frankel and Gerry were in the know that Burbank and the president were planning issuing Executive Order 127 so that no protest of environmental laws would be tolerated and those who attempt to protest would be subject to imprisonment and subjected to hard labor, a heavy fine in the six figures, and forced to help dismantle human industrial civilization.

Sherman served papers on Frankel and Gerry for inciting lawlessness, disturbing peace and order.

Damuel was in the know. He was attempting to file for Lot 21 and Judith's lot.

The two houses of Congress unable to meet the steady stream of wants of the environmentalists, executive orders from the administration, and the slow awakening of the larger citizenry, decided to go with some of the best thinking for a democracy, a return to

Jefferson, Madison, Locke and others, and put all national lands up for sale to its citizens. Thus privatizing one-third or more of the United States of America and getting it out of the control of the minority environmentalists, who can't be sataisfied and who increasingly exhibit dangerous intentions, getting laws passed to sue government at government's expense, which of course is the taxpayer's expense. Shares in public lands would be issued to every citizen. Then land would be auctioned by bidding those shares at public auction. And from there the land could be owned by citizens, cared for and managed by citizens with their natural, innate pride of ownership.

Congress had worked out its plan and gotten the mechanism set up for distributing the equal shares before they released it to the news. It was like an act of war in their secrecy. Then congress carefully released the new law to the organizations asking for help from the environmentalists over the last three decades and the environmentalists read of the land shares in the news media and were caught off guard and for a change shocked.

When the environmentalists got hold of it by reading it in the public press, it followed in their press with as usual all the Wall Street expressions so used by the environmentalists and not familiar with the ordinary citizen. They wrote and spoke of it as the greatest initial public offering, IPO, in American history. And they spoke of their options but since they hadn't purchased any options or derivatives, had never built a fence, cut a road, paid a fee, a mortgage or a tax, they had no options to exercise, none to buy or sell. The expiration date had expired. All they could claim was what they had always claimed—free land shared by no one else.

"The greatest greed I've ever witnessed all because they had no other real needs," Robert Markham observed.

Even Frankel and Gerry were caught off guard. They thought of protesting Jarvis' logging but there was no public land any more. The shares to individuals were in the mail. There would be no government to pay for having itself sued and paid for out of taxes. They had not planned for this. They did not know what individual would have what piece of land.

Sheriff Sherman put handcuffs on James and led him to the police car. Joyce and Elmer Jarvis asked permission to talk to James. They tried to comfort him and assure him that somehow he would be all right. James looked wildly at them. He was out of it.

"We'll come and see you," they promised. "We'll try to help you. These are odd times. It's hard to believe what's happening. We'll come as soon as possible."

"I hope, I think, your land and my lot are safe. Maybe we can now go on," Markham said to Judith.

"I don't know what will be coming in the mail," she said.

"Shall we rest tonight and see what happens tomorrow?" Cameron asked.

"That's about all any of us can do," said Arthur Stahlek with his arm around his mother.

"I'm ready for some quiet," Ms. Carver said.

"Just what shall we do?"

"Help the sheriff," someone said.

"By all means," said another.

"I want to spend the night with you," Markham said to Judith. "We've been through too much to keep traveling alone."

Judith nodded and moved closer and he put his arm around her.

And so passed the night.

THE END

Leota Korns

ABOUT THE AUTHOR

In 1966, newcomers to Southwest Colorado, Leota Korns and her husband, Richard, put money down on beautiful mountain property only one and a half miles from the city's limits. Their land is surrounded by thousands of acres of national forest and so near to the city. Can you imagine?

Twenty-five miles to the north are the mountains of the Continental Divide, extending around to the east and north on up the Continent. To the south and west lies the desert with over 300 square miles of Indian Ruins and always a distant range of mountains.

Growth has come and will come and so will the opposition. Out of this ongoing experience with a lawyer always a must, she has written this novel.

www.ingramcontent.com/pod-product-compliance
Lightning Source LLC
Chambersburg PA
CBHW030248290526
45785CB00001B/12